Zachary Richard Sylvain Godin Maurice Basque

Scott Long Michelle Haj-Broussard Glenda Cormier-Williams Kristi Guillory

The History of the Acadians
of Louisiana

Production team, Louisiana:

Zachary Richard, author-director
Scott Long, graphic design, layout
Kristi Guillory, research
Michelle Haj-Broussard, educational consultant
Glenda Cormier-Williams, educational consultant
Benny Graeff, illustrator
Barry Jean Ancelet, consultant
Denise Contant, translator
Georges Desjardins, translator

With the collaboration of (Chapter 1):

Rosemonde Chiasson
Sylvain Godin, historian, Village Historique Acadien
Maurice Basque, historian
Hélène Devarennes, director, École de Grande-Digue
Louise Beaulieu, professor, University of Moncton
Eric Snow, Department of Acadian Studies, University of
    Moncton
Amélie Giroux, Department of Acadian Studies, University
    of Moncton
Réjean Ouellette, text revision
Réjean Roy, graphic design, www.rejean.ca
Raymond Thériault, consultant

ISBN 978-1-935754-29-9

University of Louisiana at Lafayette Press
P.O. Box 40831
Lafayette, LA 70504
www.ulpress.org

Library of Congress Cataloging-in-Publication Data

Richard, Zachary.
[Histoire des Acadiennes et des Acadiens de la Louisiane. English]
The history of the Acadians of Louisiana / Zachary Richard,
    Sylvain Godin, Maurice Basque.
pages cm
Originally published as: Histoire des Acadiennes et des Acadiens
    de la Louisiane. c2012.
Suitable for grade 7 to 8.
Includes bibliographical references.
ISBN 978-1-935754-29-9 (pbk.)
1. Cajuns–Louisiana–History–Juvenile literature.
2. Cajuns–Louisiana–Social life and customs–Juvenile literature.
3. Louisiana–Social life and customs–Juvenile literature.
4. Louisiana–History–Juvenile literature. I. Godin, Sylvain.
II. Basque, Maurice. III. Title.
F380.A2R4713 2013
305.84'10763–dc23
                                        2013025981

Cover Illustrations:
front cover: Robert Dafford
back cover: Benny Graeff

Cover Photos:
Crawfish boil: Lucius Fontenot
Dewey Balfa: Center for Louisiana Studies
The Acadian Memorial
Mardi Gras: Lucius Fontenot
In the field: Center for Louisiana Studies

Foreword

This book is witness to the resilience of Acadian identity in Louisiana. Two hundred and forty-five years after the arrival of the first exiles along the bayous, two hundred and seven years after the territory became the eighteenth state of the United States, ninety years after the French language was banished from official discourse, there are still people in Louisiana who consider themselves Acadian and who struggle for the survival of their culture and language.

This book is also eloquent proof of the persistence of the Acadian tradition of mutual aid. Without the generous support and solidarity of the Acadian community of New Brunswick, this book would simply never have been.

A particular debt of gratitude is owed to Bernard Thériault, Mirelle Cyr, and Maurice Basque. Their encouragement was critical. Jacques and Suzanne Ouellet of the Editions du Grande Marée furnished us with the basic elements of the layout without which our boat would have never been launched. Finally, much of the content of this book is based on *Cajun Country* (University Press of Mississippi) by Barry Jean Ancelet, Glen Pitre, and Jay Edwards.

A word on vocabulary. It is not without irony that the Acadians of Louisiana are better known by the term given to us by the Anglo-Americans: Cajuns. In Louisiana French, Acadian (or Cadien) is pronounced "Kah djahn" which the Anglo-Americans modified to "Cajun." The terms can be used interchangeably: Cajun, Cadien, and Acadian all refer to the same ethnic group living in the southern parishes of Louisiana who descended from the original exiles of the Acadian Deportation.

The origin of the word "Acadie" remains a mystery. Is it in reference to the Arcadia of ancient Greece or a word derived from an Amerindian language (either Mi'kmaq or Abenaquis)? During the time of Henri IV, the colony, founded in 1604, was referred to both as "L'Acadie" and "La Cadie." For the American poet Henry Wadsworth Longfellow, whose contribution to the persistence of Acadian identity via his poem "Evangeline" was considerable, the land was called "Acadia" and the people "Acadians." One thing is certain: by the end of the nineteenth century, and particularly after the Acadian Congress of 1881, the descendants of the exiles in the Canadian maritime provinces opted definitively for the term "Acadie."

In Louisiana, however, the descendants of the exiles referred to themselves as "Cadien." In spite of being isolated from the Acadian community of Canada, the "Cajuns" were able to preserve the memory of "Acadie." The history of the Deportation and exile were passed from generation to generation, but after more than two centuries, the details were eroded away. Somehow, in spite of the absence of any formal history, the story was passed on. I heard tell of the "Grand Dérangement" from my grandparents. They could not have found Acadie on a map, however, and they had little notion of how the exiles, their ancestors, had arrived in Louisiana.

The forced removal of the Acadians was conceived by the British to destroy the land and its people. But rather than having no Acadie, today there are several. The seeds that were thrown to the wind during the Deportation took root in the Magdalen Islands, in Louisiana, on the North Shore of the Saint Lawrence, in Baie Sainte Marie and Cape Breton, Nova Scotia, on Prince Edward Island, in Maine, along the shores of the Baie des Chaleurs, and all over New Brunswick. Each one of these communities, largely isolated from the others, evolved in its own way. Each created its own traditions and wrote its own history. Local, national, and international politics have influenced the respective development of the multiple communities of Acadian heritage of the twenty-first century, as well as climate, relative isolation, interaction with neighboring ethnic groups, and other factors.

There has been no country called "Acadie" for over two hundred and fifty years. And yet Acadian identity persists. There is no Acadian passport, no political recognition. One is Acadian, or Cadien, or Cajun simply because one considers oneself to be.

In spite of the relentless pressure of cultural assimilation, the persistence of Acadian identity among the next generation of Cajuns seems to be guaranteed. Territory, worldview, heritage, and lifestyle collectively reinforce a notion of cultural solidarity even though the French language of Louisiana is spoken today only by a minority of Cajuns.

It is our hope that this book will inspire future generations to discover the heritage that it celebrates.

– Zachary Richard

VI

The Team

Zachary Richard, singer-songwriter and poet, was born in Scott, Louisiana, in 1950. His recording career spans forty years and twenty albums. Recognized as an ardent defender of the French language and culture of Acadian Louisiana, he is Officier de l'Ordre des Arts et Lettres of the French Republic, Member de l'Ordre des Francophones d'Amérique, Chevalier de l'Ordre de la Pléiade, and Member of the Order of Canada.

Michelle Haj-Broussard, Glenda Cormier-Williams, Scott Long, Kristi Guillory, Zachary Richard

Scott Long obtained his diploma in fine arts and graphic design from Louisiana State University. He is owner of LONGevity Design, specializing in website development. He has collaborated on several projects with Action Cadienne, the Acadian Memorial, and CODOFIL. A self- taught French speaker, Scott is the father of three girls enrolled in French Immersion.

Kristi Guillory is a musician, songwriter, and folklorist. She holds a B.A. in francophone studies and a masters degree in English literature from the University of Louisiana at Lafayette. Kristi collaborated in the creation of the Archives of Cajun and Creole Folklore at the Center for Louisiana Studies, overseeing the audio and video collections. She currently teaches Cajun Music at UL Lafayette.

Michelle Haj-Broussard obtained her Ph.D in education at Louisiana State University. Michelle began teaching French in 1991 and was a teacher of French Immersion for ten years. She is a board member of CODOFIL and is president of the Consortium of French Immersion schools. Michelle is a professor at McNeese State University where she teaches education, mathematics, and foreign language.

Glenda Cormier-Williams holds diplomas from the Université de Dijon (France) and McNeese State University. She has taught French Immersion and has been Director of World Languages for Calcasieu Parish. She is currently a professor at McNeese State University and a consultant in foreign language education. Glenda is the director of l'Association louisianaise des clubs de français des Écoles secondaires (ALFCES).

Table of Contents

Chapter 3

The establishment of Acadian society in Louisiana *58*

Chapter 4

The History
of the Acadians

of Louisiana

Chapter 1

The History of colonial Acadie *to the* *Deportation of 1755*

Atlantic
Ocean

Acadie

Acadie, circa 1700

© R. Roy

0   200 km

This chapter will transport you into the past, on the trails that the Acadians of Louisiana traveled. The adventure begins with the arrival of the first French explorers to Île Sainte-Croix off the coast of present-day Maine in 1604, and it continues with the settlement of the first families in 1632.

The Deportation of the Acadians, foreseen by the British as early as 1713 after the Treaty of Utrecht, was implemented in 1755. The Deportation is the most important event in the history of the Acadians. This terrible episode links all of the Acadian communities no matter where they are found, from Louisiana to the maritime provinces of Canada, on the North Shore of the Saint Lawrence River, and everywhere that descendants of the exiles proclaim their Acadian identity.

IMPORTANT DATES: FROM 1604 TO 1764

French Acadie (1604 TO 1710)

1604
A French expedition led by Pierre Du Gua de Mons crosses the Atlantic and establishes a post at Île Sainte-Croix.

1605
Due to a very harsh winter, the little colony crosses the Bay of Fundy and establishes Port-Royal.

1607
The founding of Jamestown in Virginia.

1608
The founding of Québec by Samuel de Champlain.

1632
Three hundred French settlers, the first families, arrive in Acadie.

1650
The colony grows, establishing new settlements at Grand Pré and Beaubassin.

1700
The population of Acadie is approximately 1,300 souls.

1710
Acadie falls to the British, forcing the settlers of Port-Royal to flee.

© R. Roy

1.1 An Acadian house at the end of the 18th century

The Deportation (1755 TO 1764)

1713
The Treaty of Utrecht cedes Acadie to the British Crown. It is renamed Nova Scotia.

1749
Founding of Halifax.

1750
The population of Acadie is more than 14,000.

1755
The Deportation begins.

1762
The Acadians held in Halifax are sent to Boston, where the colonial officials of Massachusetts refuse to let them disembark. They are returned to Halifax.

1763
The Treaty of Paris ends the Seven Years War, also known as the French and Indian War.

1764
The end of the Deportation.

Europeans in Acadie

In 1604, Pierre Du Gua, sieur de Mons, crossed the Atlantic Ocean at the head of a French expedition. His mandate: establish a trading post for furs in the New World. Accompanying the expedition was a cartographer, Samuel de Champlain, as well as soldiers, carpenters, blacksmiths, locksmiths, masons, and other craftsmen.

Sieur de Mons had a great project in mind: create a permanent colony in the New World. He enjoyed a monopoly of the fur trade granted by Henri IV of France. Arriving in North America, the French explored the coast of present-day Nova Scotia. Searching for a suitable place to

1.2 Pierre Du Gua de Mons

Map 1: The Atlantic Crossing

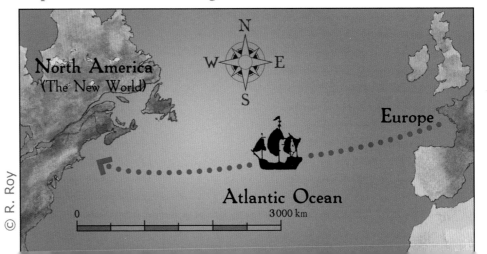

Map 2: A new territory

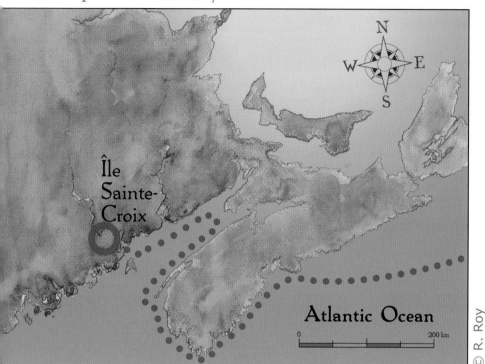

© R. Roy

NEW DISCOVERIES

Other Europeans played a significant role in the region of Île Sainte-Croix at the same time that the colony was founded by de Mons. Research one of these explorers and present his story to your class. The explorer you choose can be of any nationality.

found a settlement, they landed on an island at the mouth of a river covered by a majestic forest, the trees of which would serve as the wood for the construction of buildings. In addition, de Mons believed that the island would be protected from possible attacks by Native Americans.

Sieur de Mons gave the name Sainte-Croix (Holy Cross) to the settlement and to the river.

1.3 Samuel de Champlain

© R. Roy

1.4 A wigwam

© R. Roy

Did you know...

The "New World" refers to the lands explored by Europeans across the Atlantic Ocean from Europe, which, along with Asia, comprised the "Old World."

he first inhabitants

If the territory of Acadie was new for the Europeans, it was very well known by peoples who had inhabited North America for over 10,000 years. These peoples lived in harmony with the natural environment. Over the centuries, they had adapted to the difficult climate of the region. These Native Americans did not have the same relationship with the land as the Europeans. They believed that the land belonged to all living creatures and that human beings should share the environment with the plants and animals. The Native Americans could not conceive of owning a piece of property to the exclusion of others. The land, just like water and the air, was to be shared.

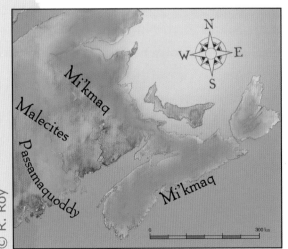

Map 3: The First Nations in Eastern Canada

The Europeans call these people "Indians" because the earliest explorers believed that they had arrived in the East Indies. Today these people are called Native Americans or First Nations.

The Native Americans whose territory was settled by de Mons were the Passamaquoddy. As early as the end of the 16th century, the Passamaquoddy had encountered Europeans. Basque fishermen as well as explorers had visited the region. The Mi'kmaq and the Malecites are the other First Nations who inhabited the area.

© R. Roy

I.5 Native Americans in birch bark canoes

The Native Americans used birch bark canoes for water travel. These canoes were light enough to be carried through the forest from one river to another, a method called portage. Native Americans housed themselves primarily in wigwams, tents of animal hides and birch bark that could easily be disassembled and transported from place to place, a system of habitation perfectly suited to the nomadic lifestyle of the First Nations.

 le Sainte-Croix

By the fall of 1604, Pierre Du Gua, sieur de Mons, and his men finished the construction of their trading post on Sainte-Croix. The expedition had carried dismantled buildings from France. Wood from the trees on the island as well as the mainland furnished all of the remaining materials necessary for the construction of the post.

NEW DISCOVERIES

Make a list of technologies and tools that were derived from the Native Americans. Explain how these technologies influenced the lives of the early European settlers in Acadie. Present your findings to your class.

Did you know...

Jacques Cartier discovered a remedy for scurvy during his second voyage to Québec in 1535-1536. The Native Americans taught him how to make a medicinal potion with bark and the leaves of certain trees.

The settlement included a warehouse for food, several houses, an oven for baking, and a mill for the grinding of grain. Since the nature of the soil was unknown to the Europeans, de Mons had several sorts of vegetables and grains planted in an effort to learn which ones would be the most productive.

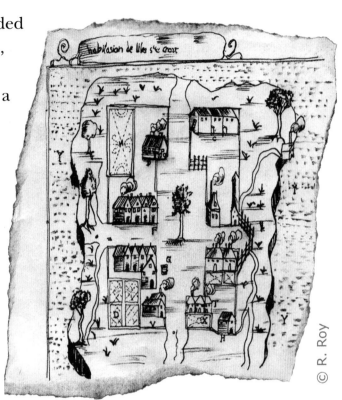

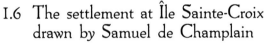

1.6 The settlement at Île Sainte-Croix drawn by Samuel de Champlain

Furs were high priced in Europe and fur trading was the main economic activity of the colony. The Europeans laid out traps hoping to capture furs. Most of the time, however, they obtained furs by trading with the Native Americans, exchanging manufactured goods such as metal pots, knives, fish hooks, and hatchets, as well as pottery and decorative beads, for furs. The Europeans also traded their baked bread for meat.

The first autumn on Saint-Croix was short. By October, snow covered the ground. Winter descended brutally on the little settlement, surprising all of the colonists. Large blocks of ice on the river prevented the Frenchmen from crossing over to the mainland. The houses were not sufficiently insulated to resist the bitter cold of the season. To make things worse, the colony ran out of firewood. The stores were frozen, and there were no vegetables or fresh fruit.

This alarming lack of nutrition led to an outbreak of scurvy. Nearly half of the men suffered. Their gums swelled so badly that they could hardly swallow. Many died. By the spring, only 44 of the original 79 men survived.

This brought the end of the settlement at Sainte-Croix. As summer approached, a better site for the trading post had to be found.

CALL TO ACTION

Using photos or illustrations downloaded from the internet, design and build a model of the French trading post at Île Sainte-Croix.

1.7 Île Sainte-Croix in the winter

© R. Roy

Port-Royal

During the summer of 1605, the French found a new site for their settlement: Port-Royal. In the southwest of present day Nova Scotia, Port-Royal enjoyed a very strategic position that allowed the observation of approaching ships at a great distance.

Map 4: Moving to Port-Royal

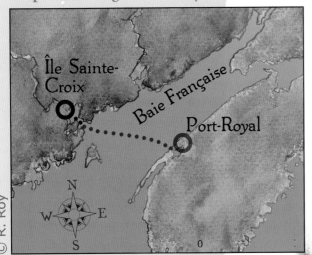

The Frenchmen pulled down several of the houses on Île Sainte-Croix and transported them to Port-Royal. Besides the houses, they built storehouses, a kitchen, and workshops. While Sainte-Croix looked like a village, Port-Royal resembled a small fort.

Life was hard at Port-Royal. During the first year, land had to be cleared and tilled, gardens planted, and preparations made for winter. In spite of all of their efforts, provisions for the following winter were still insufficient and another 12 men died of scurvy during the winter of 1605-1606.

I.8   L'habitation de Port-Royal in winter

New arrivals

During the summer of 1606, two important settlers arrived at Port-Royal: the pharmacist Louis Hébert and the lawyer Marc Lescarbot. Hébert planted a medicinal garden and gave medical care to the colonists and to the local Native Americans as well. Lescarbot was not only a lawyer but also a writer. He wrote the first history of the New World in French. He also organized a theater troupe and put on the first play in North America. Presented outdoors, *Le Théâtre de Neptune* did much to break the monotony of life at Port-Royal. It is interesting to note that several of the roles were played by Native Americans.

© R. Roy

I.9 Marc Lescarbot

The following winters were not as harsh. In the course of the winter of 1606-1607, Samuel de Champlain organized *L'Ordre du Bon Temps* (the Order of Good Times). This was, in fact, a social club created to foster good cheer in the face of very limited provisions, the harsh climate, and the homesickness that pervaded the colony.

Each member of L'Ordre organized a banquet using the means at hand. Moose, deer, caribou, rabbit, and wild goose, as well as wild berries and vegetables from the

CALL TO ACTION

Find some illustrations of Port-Royal or some photos of the present-day reconstruction. Compare the settlement of Port-Royal with that of Île Sainte-Croix. How were the two settlements different? How were they alike?

YOUR POINT OF VIEW

What are the advantages of creating a social club in a new settlement?

I.10 A Jesuit missionary meets Native Americans

Did you know...

Québec City was founded by Samuel de Champlain in 1608, four years after the founding of Sainte-Croix and one year after that of Jamestown.

garden were prepared with the greatest care. Competition developed to see who served the most delicious meals. L'Ordre du Bon Temps contributed significantly to a more healthy diet, to a feeling of camaraderie, and to a feeling that somehow Port-Royal was home.

A period of uncertainty

In spite of the construction of Port-Royal, the development of the little colony progressed very slowly. Only a few men lived in separate houses and did some farming. Rivalries in the community slowed its development. Jesuit missionaries, sent to evangelize the Native Americans, were unsatisfied with the situation at Port-Royal, and they traveled farther south to found a new settlement, Saint-Sauveur, in present-day Maine. The lack of cooperation between the colonists prevented the creation of a strong community.

The English established Jamestown in Virginia in 1607. They were concerned by the French colony in Acadie. Relations between England and France were uncertain at best, and the English felt threatened by the French colony. The English perceived the expansion of Acadie as a menace.

Geographically, Acadie was situated between New England and New France (Québec). For many years, both England and France claimed the territory. In 1613, sailing from Virginia, Samuel Argall attacked Saint-Sauveur and Port-Royal, destroying them both. A few years later, William Alexander installed a small group of colonists at Port-Royal. In honor of his native land, he named the little colony Nova Scotia (New Scotland). Alexander's efforts to develop the colony did not bear fruit. The French soon reclaimed the territory and drove the Scots off. These skirmishes marked the beginning of a long series of conflicts that afflicted the colony from 1613 to 1710.

CALL TO ACTION

Plan a banquet for L'Ordre du Bon Temps. Prepare a menu and organize some social activities. Compare your plans with those of your classmates.

Map 5: New France, New England, and l'Acadie

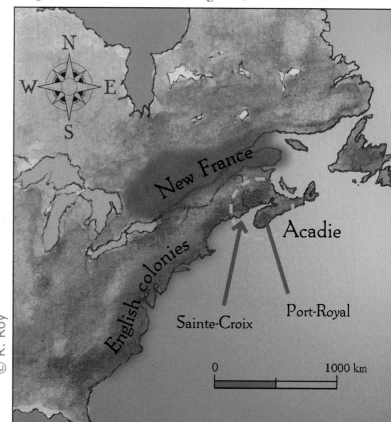

© R. Roy

The first French pioneers in Acadie

In spite of all of their efforts, during the early years of the settlement the French were unable to find enough colonists to assure the survival of the colony. Before 1632, less than 300 souls arrived from France. Shortly thereafter the first pioneer families arrived. The children of these families were the earliest Acadians, the first to be born in the New World.

Internal conflicts marked the beginning of the colony. Two French *seigneurs* vied for control: Charles de Saint-Étienne de la Tour and Charles de Menou d'Aulnay. De la Tour established himself at the mouth of the Saint John's River on the site of present-day Saint Johns. D'Aulnay resided at Port-Royal. For years, these two men were at war. In 1645, d'Aulnay attacked the fortress of de la Tour, who was absent at the time. De la Tour's wife, Françoise-Marie Jacquelin, led the defense of the fort but was defeated. With d'Aulnay's victory, de la Tour fled to Québec. D'Aulnay's victorious reign was short lived, however. He died in 1650 at Port-Royal in a canoeing accident.

After 1650, Acadie developed rapidly thanks to the growth of the settlers' families, each of which typically contained six or seven children and often more. The quality of life

Did you know...

From 1604 to 1710, Acadie had two administrative systems. From 1604 to 1670, Acadie was administered by companies of trade. The control and the financing of the colony were in the hands of merchants who received their authority from the King. From 1670 to 1710, the colony was administered by the royal government. Under this arrangement, King Louis XIV named the governors who ruled the colony in the name of the King.

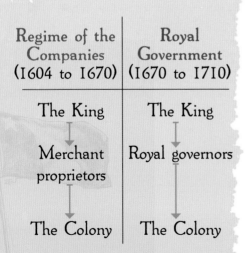

Regime of the Companies (1604 to 1670)	Royal Government (1670 to 1710)
The King ↓	The King ↓
Merchant proprietors ↓	Royal governors ↓
The Colony	The Colony

and life expectancy were greater in Acadie than in France. Most of the residents were farmers or laborers. When children became old enough to start their own families, new lands had to be cleared. The second generation of Acadians was as prolific as the first and had large families. On average, women married at twenty-one and men at twenty-six. New villages were founded as the area around Port-Royal was no longer sufficient to provide for the rapidly growing population.

© R. Roy

I.II Françoise-Marie Jacquelin

Map 6: England and France

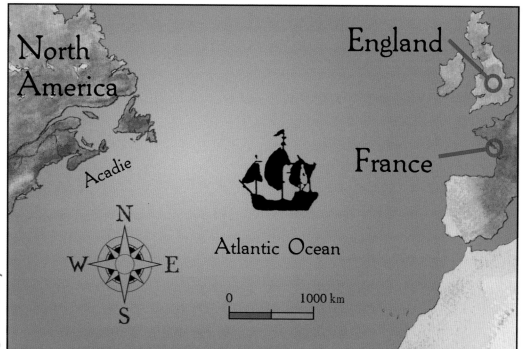

© R. Roy

Did you know...

In the seventeenth century, Acadie had no precise boundaries.

During this period, England and France often went to war. Both European powers coveted the colony. Sometimes the British ruled the colony and sometimes the French. The frequent changes of government were difficult for the Acadians, which is part of the reason that new villages were founded far from Port-Royal: to escape the control of whoever was at the fort.

The new settlements were north of Port-Royal along the upper reaches of the Baie Française (Bay of Fundy). Rivière-aux-Canards, Grand Pré, and Pisiguit were

Map 7: The new Acadian villages

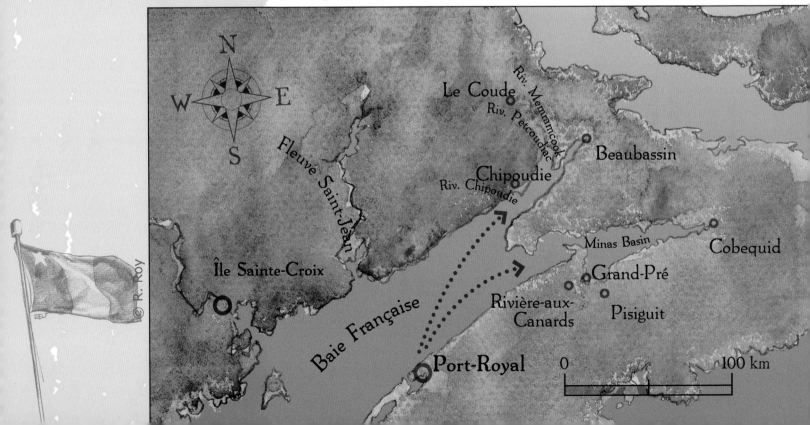

founded along the Minas Basin (le basin des Mines) with Cobequid on its upper reaches. These areas were at the heart of colonial Acadie and were rich farmlands. The ancestors of many Acadian families such as Boudreau, Daigle, Doucet, Gaudet, Hébert, Landry, LeBlanc, Melanson, Poirier, Robichaud, Thériault, and Thibodeau thrived in these communities.

Other families settled farther north on the isthmus of Chignectou at the end of the Bay of Fundy. Like the families of the Minas Basin, they chose their sites because of the fertility of the soil and the possibility of living in peace. Chipoudie was founded on the western shore of the Bay of Fundy. Not only was the site secluded and the land fertile, but it was at the confluence of three rivers: the Chipoudie, the Petcoudiac (Petitcodiac), and the Memramcook. It was therefore a very favorable location for trade, particularly the fur trade with the Mi'kmaqs.

Other Acadian families settled ever farther from Port-Royal along the Petcoudiac River. The entire region was inhabited by pioneering Acadian families: Blanchard, Comeau, Landry, Léger, Saulnier, Savoie, and others. These settlements lined the Petcoudiac up to le Coude (the elbow), the area around present-day Moncton.

YOUR POINT OF VIEW

Why do you think the first Acadian families settled near water? Examine a map of New Brunswick, Canada, to see if the Acadian settlements were always established near water. How did the proximity to bodies of water affect housing and nutrition, as well as the occupations of the early Acadians?

Did you know...

The soil of the dried salt marshes in Acadie was five times more productive than that of the fields inland. Cabbage, beets, onions, carrots, turnips, and other vegetables were grown in abundance in the dried saltwater marsh. After the marsh was protected by the dikes, it would take five to seven years before the salt was leached out sufficiently to allow farming. Once this was accomplished, these fields were the most productive in North America at the time.

Les aboiteaux

The presence of tidal marshes was foremost in the choice of settlement sites in the regions where new villages were founded away from Port-Royal. In order to feed their families and livestock, the Acadians dried the salt marshes that line the Bay of Fundy. The lands thus reclaimed were planted with vegetables for the settlers and hay for sheep and cattle.

In order to prevent the Bay of Fundy's tides, the highest in the world, from flooding the marshes, the Acadians built dikes using tree trunks and soil. These dikes were pierced at regular

I.12 The building of an aboiteau

intervals by wooden sluice gates known as aboiteaux. Through the aboiteaux, fresh water from upland would flow out into the bay. The aboiteaux had a wooden gate on the side of the bay. This gate would open at low tide under the pressure of the water flowing from the fields. The rising tide would close the gate, thus preventing salt water from flowing into the dried marsh. The term **aboiteau** referred to the entire system: the dike, the dried marsh, as well as the sluice gate itself. Thanks to this remarkable engineering, Acadian families reaped the bounty of the tidal marsh. The hay grown there was indispensable in feeding the livestock in winter.

NEW DISCOVERIES

The Acadians built the aboiteaux in order to exploit the tidal marshes. Build a model of an aboiteau with modeling clay and various materials such as sticks and balsa wood.

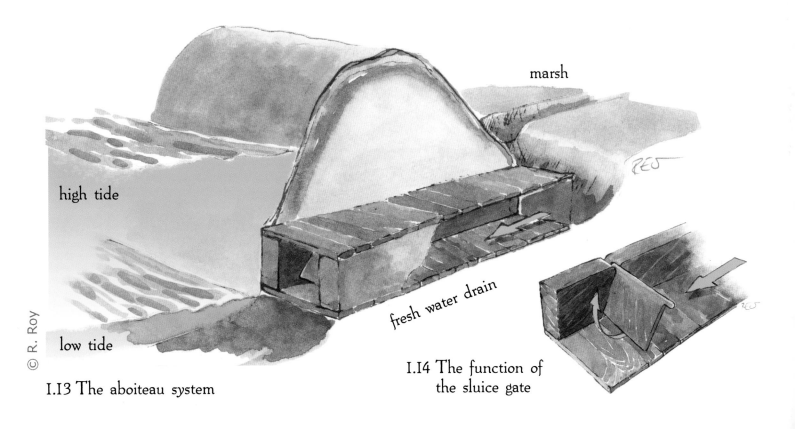

© R. Roy

high tide

low tide

marsh

fresh water drain

I.13 The aboiteau system

I.14 The function of the sluice gate

Daily life

In every Acadian village were found various craftsmen: blacksmiths, barrel makers, carpenters, cabinet builders. Mid-wives helped women to deliver their babies. Folk healers known as **guérisseurs** practiced traditional healing using remedies brought from France or learned from the Native Americans.

The survival of the Acadian homestead depended on the efforts of all of the members of the family—the father, the mother, and the children. From the youngest to the oldest, all contributed to the numerous daily activities necessary to feed the family and maintain the home.

Did you know...
Around 1700, approximately 1,300 Acadians lived in the colony. By 1750, the population had grown to nearly 14,000.

© R. Roy

1.15 A barrel maker

1.16 A cabinet maker

1.17 A spinning wheel

When the father of the house was not occupied with fishing or working in the fields, he would be employed at other labors such as taking in firewood and making repairs on the farmstead. The mother was the heart of the home. Besides taking care of the children and of the house, she would make clothes for the entire family. For this, she had to know how to spin, sew, and knit. She would also prepare meat, clean fish, make preserves of fruits and vegetables, and cook the meals. On top of this, she would lend a hand in tending the crops in the field and maintain the vegetable garden.

© R. Roy

I.18 Preparing wool

I.19 Children share in household tasks

From very early ages, the children participated in household tasks. This apprenticeship began with simple chores such as feeding the animals, bringing in firewood, or washing the dishes. Nonetheless, the children had plenty of time for playing with homemade toys.

VHA

Life before the Deportation

Relations between the French colony of Acadie and the British colonies of New England constantly changed. Sometimes the colonies engaged in trade. Other times they confronted one another militarily. During this period, France and England often were at war, and the effects of these wars were felt in North America. The British in New England used the pretext of war in Europe to attack the Acadian settlements and menaced Acadie constantly. In 1690, military expeditions from New England burned Port-Royal and Beaubassin. The Acadian families suffered greatly from these incursions, and the period was very difficult for many Acadians. After the British attacks, they had to begin their lives anew, starting from scratch. There were few French soldiers to protect the colony.

In 1710, French Acadie fell permanently to the British. The British renamed Port-Royal Annapolis Royal in honor of Queen Anne

Map 8: The British and French colonies before 1755

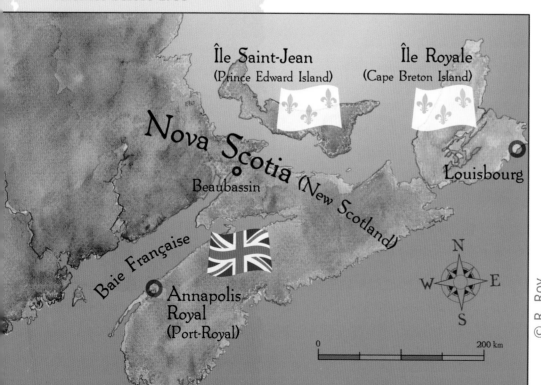

Île Saint-Jean
(Prince Edward Island)

Île Royale
(Cape Breton Island)

Nova Scotia (New Scotland)

Beaubassin

Louisbourg

Baie Française

Annapolis Royal (Port-Royal)

N
W   E
S

© R. Roy

0   200 km

of England. In 1713, France and England signed a treaty of peace at Utrecht, the Netherlands. Under the terms of the treaty, Acadie became a British colony with the name "Nova Scotia." France also lost Newfoundland and Hudson Bay to the British. Île Royale (Cape Breton) and Île Saint-Jean (Prince Edward Island) remained French. France maintained fishing rights along the Newfoundland coast and the right to dry the catch on the west coast of the island, which came to be known as the "French Shore."

The Acadians found themselves living in a colony administered by the British. The great majority of the population, however, remained French. The English in Nova Scotia comprised only a small group of administrators, military personnel, merchants, and fishermen.

NEW DISCOVERIES

There are place names in Louisiana that are derived from Acadie. On a map of Louisiana, find the names of these villages or regions. On a map of North America find the places in Acadie (Nova Scotia and New Brunswick) which have the same names as places in Louisiana.

I.20 The port of Louisbourg

© R. Roy

Relations with the British authorities

From 1713, the British governed Nova Scotia. The governor of the colony answered to the British King and his ministers in council. For the Acadians, the priorities were to conserve their way of life and to practice the Catholic religion. During this period, Protestantism dominated Great Britain and Catholics had few rights under the British government.

Over time, the British governors became more and more demanding of the Acadians. They demanded that the Acadians sign an oath of allegiance to the British crown. Most of the Acadians accepted under two conditions: the free practice of their Catholic faith and, in case of war, the exemption from having to bear arms. To fight for the British would mean fighting against the French and against the Native American allies of the French. The British did not have the military force to impose the oath of allegiance and grudgingly accepted the neutrality of the Acadians, whom they referred to as "French Neutrals."

The beginning of the end

The British authorities in Nova Scotia were anxious that the territory be populated with reliable British subjects. Their hopes of converting the Acadians to the Protestant religion and forcing them to become loyal subjects of the British

crown failed in the face of Acadian intractability. In order
to ensure that reliable subjects inhabited the colony, they
sought Protestant colonists. Authorities in London eventually
sent more than 2,000 colonists from Europe. In 1749, the
British founded Halifax. This Anglo-Protestant city eventually
became the capital of Nova Scotia, supplanting Annapolis
Royal. The location of Halifax on the eastern coast gave the
British a military base for operations against Louisbourg, the
French fortress on Île Royale.

The new colonists settled not only at Halifax, but also at
Dartmouth and Lunenburg. Edward Cornwallis, founder
of Halifax and governor of Nova Scotia from 1749 to 1752,
intended to do away with Acadian neutrality. He attempted to
force them to take an unconditional oath of allegiance.

YOUR POINT OF VIEW

The Acadians adopted a policy
of political neutrality. Have you
ever tried to remain neutral in
a quarrel between two of your
friends? What means did you
take to remain neutral? How
did you feel and what was the
reaction of your friends?

This oath would oblige the
Acadians to bear arms in the
event of a military conflict, and
thus to fight against the French
and their Native American
allies. The Acadians refused.

The founding of Halifax
increased the British
population of Nova Scotia
considerably. The Acadians
viewed this development
with trepidation, realizing

Map 9: Halifax and the British and French forts

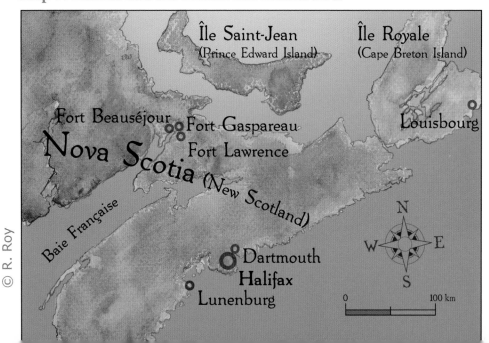

© R. Roy

that the dominance of Anglo-British subjects was a direct
threat to their way of life. Many Acadians moved to the
French colony of Île Saint-Jean (Prince Edward Island) or
along the Petcoudiac, Memramcook, and Saint-Jean rivers in
French controlled territory. The French constructed forts at
Beauséjour and Gaspareau on the Chignectou Isthmus.

The French forts in the Chignectou Isthmus were a
counterpoint to the British Fort Lawrence. In addition to
building the forts, the French government ordered the
burning of the Acadian settlements at Beaubassin in 1750,
forcing the Acadians to resettle in French territory. This was
the beginning of the ***Grand Dérangement***.

Bibliothèque et Archives Canada

1.21 The port of Halifax, circa 1796

The Deportation

During the 1750s, tension between the British and the French increased in North America. In June of 1755, a British military expedition, commanded by Lieutenant Colonel Robert Moncton, attacked the French forts Beauséjour and Gaspareau. When the French commander surrendered, the British found Acadian militiamen inside the fort. They declared to Moncton that the French had forced them to bear arms, and Moncton pardoned them.

However, the governor of Nova Scotia, Charles Lawrence, saw things in a different light. According to Lawrence, the fact that the Acadians were captured in the fort proved that they were not "neutral." He revoked the pardon granted by Moncton and convened a meeting of the Council of Nova Scotia. On July 28, 1755, approximately one hundred Acadian delegates appeared before the Council. They refused once again to swear an unconditional oath of allegiance to the British crown.

The Council ordered that the Acadian delegates be taken prisoner, proclaimed the confiscation of all of the goods and properties of the Acadians, and decreed their expulsion from Nova Scotia. The Deportation had begun.

© R. Roy

I.22 Charles Lawrence

In the fall of 1755, Charles Lawrence ordered that the expulsion orders be enforced. The Acadian families of the area near Fort Beauséjour were the first to be deported.

One of the most infamous episodes of the Deportation took place at Grand-Pré. John Winslow, the British commanding officer there, called all of the men and boys over ten years old to a meeting at the church. While the Acadians were in the church, they were taken captive. They were told that all of their goods and properties were confiscated and that they were to be deported with their families.

During the Deportation, no Acadian families were sent to Louisiana. The exiles were sent to the British North American colonies in an effort to assimilate them. The Acadians were known to be hardworking people and the British hoped to convert them into faithful subjects.

Map 10: The Acadian Deportation

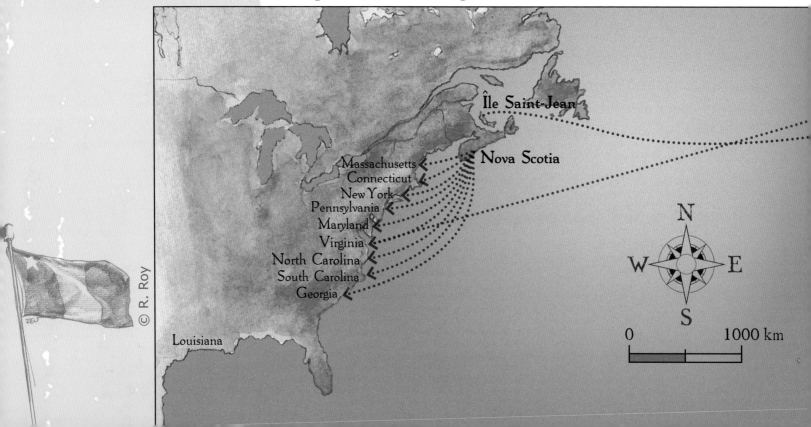

© R. Roy

The British forced several thousand Acadians—men, women, and children—onto transport ships and sent them to the British North American colonies. The authorities in Nova Scotia failed to inform their fellow administrators of the Deportation, and the Acadians arrived unannounced, surprising the local authorities everywhere they landed. Many Acadians refused to embark. These Acadians were hunted down like rebels and traitors. The British authorities in Nova Scotia sought to rid the colony of the Acadians completely. In their eyes, the Acadians constituted a potential threat in the war being prepared against the French.

England

France

1.23 The Deportation

© R. Roy

Chapter 2

Exile:

scattered to the wind

Crammed into the dank, dark holds of the small British transports, given substandard food and water, and denied knowledge of their destination, the Acadian deportees were a miserable lot. As an Acadian exiled to Pennsylvania recalled: "We were so crowded on the transport ships, that we had not room even for all our bodies to lay down, and consequently were prevented from carrying with us the basic necessities." The British ships carried approximately one-third more passengers than they were designed to hold. The ships' stores were rapidly depleted. Overcrowding and poor diet exacerbated by the stress and seasickness that plagued the voyage had devastating effects on the health of the exiles. Epidemics of typhus and smallpox broke out.

IMPORTANT DATES: FROM 1755 TO 1809

1755
The Deportation of the Acadians begins in July. The first deportees are 22 men considered the most dangerous by the British authorities. They are sent from Beaubassin to South Carolina.

1757
The colonial assembly of Pennsylvania decrees that Acadian parents are obliged to apprentice their children to Anglo-American masters.

1761
Captain Roderick MacKenzie attacks an Acadian village in the Straights of Northumberland (Baie Verte). He captures 787 persons. 335 are taken to Halifax in detention. The others are freed and remain in their settlements.

1763
The British authorities allow Acadians to remain in Nova Scotia under the condition that they swear an oath of allegiance to the British crown.

1764
Acadians arrive in Saint Domingue to settle on land that was promised to them by French authorities. They are to work on the construction of the naval base at Mole Saint-Nicolas.

1765
A group of 193 Acadians led by Joseph Broussard, dit Beausoleil, arrives at the port of New Orleans in February.

Against the Tide

2.1 Acadians imprisoned in England

NEW DISCOVERIES

Can you find other groups of people who lived through a similar ordeal as the deported Acadians, either during the same period or more recently?

1765

The Foreign Minister of France, Étienne-François de Choiseul, sends a small group of Acadians to settle on Belle-Île-en-Mer off the coast of Brittany. The colony does not prosper and most of the Acadians ultimately depart for Louisiana.

1765

Exiled Acadians settle in Québec. Over 2,000 arrive from New England.

1767

Several letters sent from the Acadian community in Louisiana circulate among the exiles in Maryland and Pennsylvania. The letters invite Acadians to come to Louisiana.

1768

About 200 Acadian men descend on New Orleans and take part in an insurrection that forces the Spanish governor to leave the colony.

1785

The great majority of the Acadian exiles living in France, 1,596 persons, immigrate en masse to Louisiana.

1809

Fleeing the Haitian Revolution, Acadians arrive in New Orleans.

The Acadians are greeted with hostility

2.2 Acadian exiles arrive in Boston

Against the Tide

The arrival of the Acadian exiles in the British North American seaports was a suprise to the local authorities. They had not been forewarned by the government of Nova Scotia. Colonial governors were stunned by the arrival of the destitute refugees. Without instructions from British colonial authorities, the local officials reacted with hostility. Although war between England and France had yet to be officially declared, the Acadians arrived in the British-American seaports in the midst of a wave of anti-French propaganda, much of it directed against Nova Scotia's Acadian population. The refugees were distrusted at best and hated at worst for their French culture and Catholic beliefs. Of all of their trials, however, none was more difficult to bear than the forced removal of their children. Many of them would be indentured to Anglo-American masters in a deliberate attempt to destroy their culture.

■ Massachusetts

The first Acadians arrived in Boston on November 12, 1755, and within a week there were over 2,000 refugees aboard ships in the harbor. Smallpox decimated their numbers. The Massachusetts government was preoccupied with controlling the exiles and was hardly concerned about their welfare. Refugee families were sent throughout the colony, each township expected to provide housing and supplies, but only during the first winter. Afterwards, the Acadians were fully expected to fare for themselves. Trained as farmers, the Acadians did not possess skills adapted to the economy of the colony. Local authorities had the power to bind out the Acadians to local masters. Local ships' captains were prohibited from hiring Acadians. They were forbidden to leave the corporate limits of the towns to which they had been assigned under penalty of flogging.

CALL TO ACTION

On a world map, indicate the places to which the Acadians were deported. On a second map, indicate the places that the descendants of the exiles live today. In comparing the two maps, what conclusions can you draw?

Against the Tide

2.4 Acadians in exile

© Robert Dafford

2.3 Acadians in the port of Boston, 1755

Did you know...

Signed in 1763, the Treaty of Paris ended the Seven Years War. The Acadians who had been detained in the British North American colonies were free to depart. Learning that Acadians had settled in Louisiana, exiles in Maryland and Pennsylvania left for there. Approximately 1,000 Acadians from these two colonies arrived in Louisiana between 1765 and 1775.

The regimentation of the Acadians was greatly relaxed by the Massachusetts government at the end of the war in 1763. British authorities in Canada agreed to allow Acadians to immigrate provided they swear an unconditional oath of allegiance. The few Acadians who could afford ships' passage sailed for Québec. The remainder began an arduous trek north, walking for months. Their original homeland now occupied by British colonists, some Acadians settled in the unoccupied lands of the Petit Codiac Valley. Many continued on to Québec.

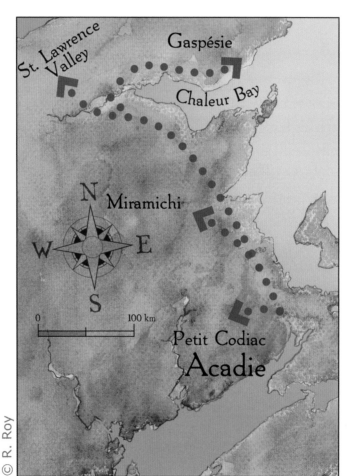

Map 11: The return of Acadians from exile

■ Maryland

The first Acadian exiles arrived in Maryland in late September 1755 aboard four dreadfully overcrowded transports. They demanded that the government recognize their status as prisoners of war and provide for their welfare. The government refused. They were forced into the open, huddled together in the snow-covered countryside, until shelter could be found. Obliged to make their own way, the Acadians grudgingly accepted low paying and often degrading work offered by their reluctant hosts.

Against the Tide

2.5 Living in wretched conditions, the Acadians fall victim to disease

© Benny Graeff

2.6 A group of Acadians huddle in the snow

Oxford Township

2.7 Philadelphia in 1755

Did you know...

After the Seven Years War, the Acadians in the British North American colonies struggled to re-establish their communities. Those in the northern colonies attempted to return to Acadie or migrate to Québec, often on foot. Those in the southern colonies disappeared without a trace. The Acadians in Pennsylvania and Maryland departed in small groups to Louisiana from the ports of Baltimore and Philadelphia.

◼ Pennsylvania

The Acadian experience in Pennsylvania resembled closely that in Maryland. Most rural townships refused to accept the exiles. The Acadians resisted being separated from one another as best they could. They concentrated in the slums of Philadelphia, surviving on charity. In January 1757, the colonial assembly passed a bill that required Acadian parents to apprentice their children to Anglo-American artisans. The children would be educated in the English language. After the war, most of the Pennsylvania Acadians joined their friends and families from Maryland and immigrated to Louisiana.

© Robert Dafford

2.8 Acadians in quarantine on Ship Island, 1755

■ South Carolina

In South Carolina, hundreds of Acadians were forced to remain aboard the transports until local authorities decided what should be done with them. The health conditions aboard the transports were so appalling that the Acadians were finally herded onto the beach. They were encouraged to depart on merchant vessels bound for England. Instead, the exiles attempted to escape into the interior. Fearing that they would join the hostile Indian tribes to the west, the South Carolina government recaptured them. Thirty Acadians were able to escape detention and disappeared. A final contingent made its way to the Santee River and set out for the French stronghold at Fort Duquesne in present day Pennsylvania. Only two of them arrived.

CALL TO ACTION

On a map of the United States, trace a route from Charleston, South Carolina, to Pittsburgh, Pennsylvania. Imagine making this trek through the woods on foot. This is the voyage that thirty Acadians attempted to make in 1755.

2.9 Acadians take flight

© Benny Graeff

Did you know...

Before the Deportation, Acadian merchants traded via sea routes. Trading with the English in Boston and with the French at Louisbourg, a group of experienced Acadian sailors plied the waters of the Baie Française (Bay of Fundy) transporting raw materials from Acadie.

On the return voyage, they brought back manufactured products, utensils, hardware, cloth, and rum.

South Carolina was as anxious to be rid of the Acadians as the Acadians were to flee. A large number of them departed on two leaky vessels, sailing into unknown waters, attempting to return to Nova Scotia. They were forced to land at Hampton Roads in Virginia. There they pooled their resources and purchased a new ship to continue their odyssey. For two months, the Acadians worked to repair their ship before setting sail and eventually arriving in the Saint John Valley of present day New Brunswick. There they joined Charles des Champs de Boishébert in his fight against the British. The remaining Acadians in Georgia and South Carolina were dispersed in the coastal counties, never to be heard from again.

2.10 Acadians negotiate the purchase of a vessel in Charleston

© Benny Graeff

■ Virginia

Virginia received the largest number of exiles, over 1,500. Virginia refused to allow the Acadians to disembark. For months, they remained stranded on board the transports before finally being sent to England. Imprisoned in the ports of Brighton, Southampton, and Liverpool, these exiles watched helplessly as their friends and family were decimated by disease. By the end of the war, half of them had perished. While in prison, they received a visit from M. de la Rochette, secretary of the French minister plenipotentiary. Moved by pity, he circulated a letter among them promising that they would be removed to France where "your treatment will be more advantageous than you expect." News of this letter spread throughout the exile communities of the Atlantic basin, creating false hopes.

CALL TO ACTION

Use a map to calculate the distance between Nova Scotia and Virginia, then from Virginia to Southampton, England. From there to Cherbourg, France, and finally to Belle-Île-en-mer. This is the journey that many Acadians made during the Deportation. How many miles total is this trip? How many kilometers? Calculate the distance from Nantes, France, to New Orleans. Add this number to the previous total. This total figure was the voyage of the Acadians who arrived in Louisiana in 1785.

2.11 Acadians imprisoned in England, 1759

© Robert Dafford

2.12 Étienne-François
de Choiseul

Étienne-François de
Choiseul, duc de
Choiseul, comte de
Stainville was effecti-
vely the prime minister
to Louis XV between
1758 and 1770. His
role on the political
and diplomatic scene
in France and in
Europe made him one
of the most important
men of state of the
eighteenth century.

■ France

At the end of the war, the exiles imprisoned in England were indeed sent to France, but their dreams of special treatment and resettlement on fertile land were shattered. They arrived in the ports of Western France to live in squalor, many of them living in the streets. Finally, in 1765, the French minister of state, Etienne François de Choiseul, established a small group of Acadians at Belle-Île-en-Mer, a small windswept island off the coast of Brittany. The colony endured but did not prosper. With little prospects of sustaining a growing community, many of the Acadians at Belle-Île would eventually immigrate to Louisiana in 1785.

2.13 Belle-Île-en-Mer

Following the fall of Louisbourg in 1758, the British invaded the Acadian stronghold of Île Saint-Jean. Of the approximately 5,000 Acadians residing there, fully two-thirds were deported to France. Those remaining fled to Québec or Saint Pierre et Miquelon. A small number were able to avoid detection and remained on the island for the duration of the war. Two of the transport ships carrying the Acadians to France, the *Violet* and the *Duke William*, were lost at sea with the death of all aboard, including over 400 Acadians.

© Gerard Braud

2.14 The port of Louisbourg

R. Roy

Map 12: Distribution of the Deportees

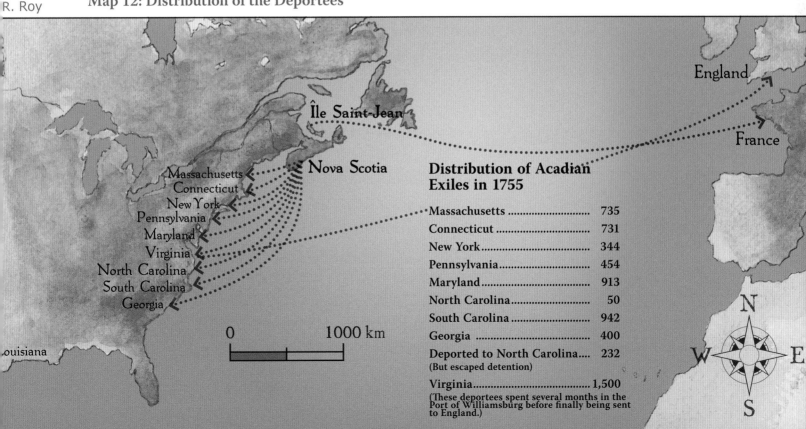

Distribution of Acadian Exiles in 1755

Massachusetts	735
Connecticut	731
New York	344
Pennsylvania	454
Maryland	913
North Carolina	50
South Carolina	942
Georgia	400
Deported to North Carolina.... (But escaped detention)	232
Virginia	1,500

(These deportees spent several months in the Port of Williamsburg before finally being sent to England.)

0   1000 km

2.15 Acadians on the island of Saint-Domingue, 1764

© Robert Dafford

◼️ Saint-Domingue

At the end of the Seven Years War, French minister of state Étienne François de Choiseul determined to rebuild French naval power in the Caribbean and saw the exiled Acadians as a potential source of labor for the construction of a naval base at Môle Saint-Nicolas. To encourage Acadian participation in this operation, the French government secretly employed a recruiting agent in New York by the name of Hanson. He circulated a proclamation on June 26, 1764, by Charles-Henri, comte d'Estaing, governor of Saint-Domingue, that promised the Acadians land and support until they became self-sufficient.

Map 13: Saint-Domingue

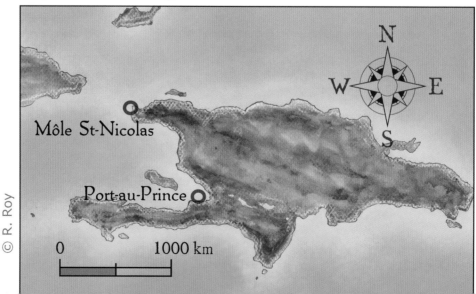

Môle St-Nicolas

Port-au-Prince

0   1000 km

© R. Roy

© Peter Glogg

2.16 Santiago de Cuba

2.17 The Haitian Revolution

January Suchodolski

The first contingent of Acadian workers in Haiti arrived on February 2, 1764, from New England. To their dismay, they were treated as forced laborers. Tropical diseases took a dramatic toll. Of the 938 Acadians sent to Môle Saint-Nicolas in 1764, only 672 remained the next year. After sustaining frightful losses to disease and malnutrition, the Acadians gradually adapted to their surroundings, integrating into the social system of this island as plantation laborers, artisans, managers, and occasionally as plantation owners. Fleeing the Haitian Revolution, many migrated to Santiago de Cuba and from there to New Orleans in 1809.

2.18 Death of Montcalm on the
Plains of Abraham

Did you know...

Many Acadians participated in the Battle of the Plains of Abraham on September 13, 1759. While the French fled the field of battle in disorder, a group of two hundred militiamen, including Acadians, resisted with valor the British forces, allowing the French to reach the Saint Charles River without great loss.

◼ Québec

The first Acadians to arrive in Québec fled the deportation of 1755, marching through the forest via Madawaska and Notre Dame du Portage. Others arrived by ship in 1756. Famine and small pox decimated their numbers. Acadian men participated in the Battle of the Plains of Abraham, a group of them protecting the retreat of the French army. After the battle, many Acadians immigrated to Bécancour and Trois-Rivières, fleeing the British army. Their status as "refugees" made them particularly vulnerable since they were officially British subjects and could be exchanged as prisoners of war.

Map 14: The St. Lawrence Valley

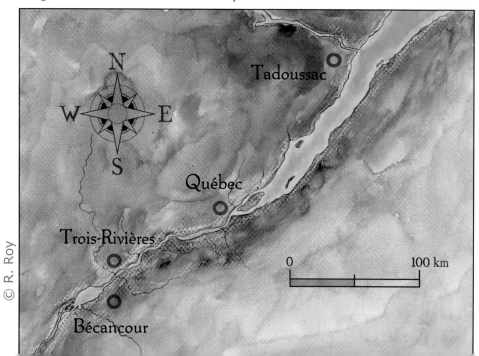

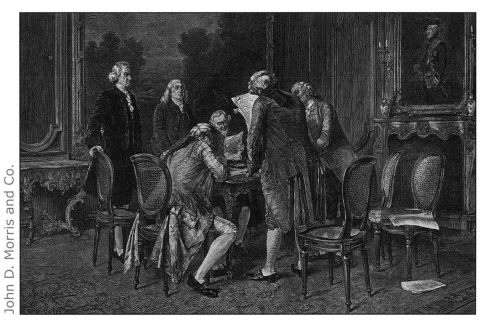

John D. Morris and Co.

2.19 Negotiation of the Treaty of Paris, 1763

CALL TO ACTION

Using the telephone directory available at www.Canada411.ca, count the number of Acadian family names in Québec City. Estimate the percentage of Québec City's population of people with Acadian family names. Do the same for the villages of Bécancour and Saint Grégoire.

Seiler

2.20 The Treaty of Paris

The second wave of Acadian immigration to Québec followed the Treaty of Paris and the end of hostilities. The exiles arrived from New England via the Saint Lawrence or via the inland route on foot through the forest. The British governor of Canada, General Murray, accepted their request to settle, requiring in exchange that they swear an oath of allegiance. 1765 marked the beginning of the permanent establishment of the Acadians in Québec with as many as 2,000 arriving from New England. Today, at least one million Québécois have Acadian family names and one in three has an Acadian ancestor.

Did you know...

Fleeing the Deportation, many Acadians took refuge on the banks of the Miramichi River at a place they called le Camp de l'Espérance (the Camp of Hope). According to the priest who accompanied them, Abbé le Geurne, the exiles were obliged to eat the leather of their shoes to stay alive during the winter of 1756. It is estimated that more than 6,000 Acadians passed through the camp between 1756 and 1770, including Beausoleil Broussard. Le Camp de l'Espérance was the center of Acadian resistance during the dispersal.

■ Acadie

Not all of the Acadians were deported during the Derangement. Some remained stubbornly on their farmsteads at Memramcook, Cocagne, Miramichi, Restigouche, Caraquet, and Nepisiguit in present-day New Brunswick. Their continued presence attracted the unwelcome attention of the British, and in October 1761, Captain Roderick MacKenzie raided numerous coastal settlements, taking 787 prisoners. Of these, 335 were removed to Halifax; the remainder, however, were permitted to stay. A sufficient number of Acadians remained to insure the viability of these settlements. They would become the basis of the Acadian society of New Brunswick once settlement was sanctioned in 1764.

Map 15: Acadian communities of New Brunswick

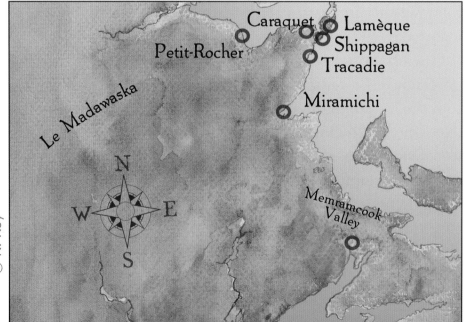

◼ Louisiana

In November 1764, a group of Acadians led by Joseph Broussard, dit Beausoleil, sailed from the port of Halifax. These Acadians had been held in detention, many forced to work on maintaining the dikes that were now in the hands of English farmers. Refusing to swear allegiance to the British crown, they were permitted by the Treaty of Paris to travel to French territory. Hiring a ship with their own money, they sailed to Haiti. There they hoped to reunite with their friends and relatives and to migrate en masse to Québec via the Mississippi Valley. However, the Saint-Domingue Acadians had been decimated by disease and the Halifax Acadians continued their journey, arriving at the port of New Orleans in February 1765. They were 193 people with little more than the clothes on their backs.

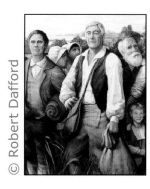

© Robert Dafford

2.22 Beausoleil arrives in Louisiana

Joseph Broussard's commitment to the French cause was unbending. In 1748, the governor of Massachusetts declared him an outlaw for his pro-French activities. In June 1755, Beausoleil and several hundred other Acadians took part in the battle of Fort Beauséjour. After the French defeat, he continued his armed struggle, harassing the British. Without the means to feed his family, he was forced to surrender in the fall of 1760. A fighter to the end, he brought his people to Louisiana, where they founded a New Acadie. Beausoleil died in Louisiana in October 1765.

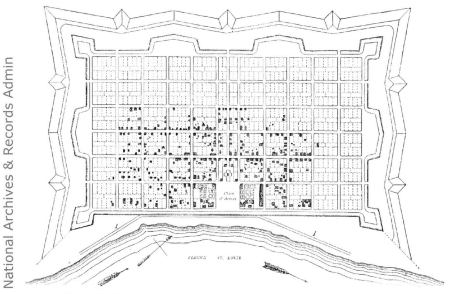

National Archives & Records Admin

2.21 New Orleans, 1763

2.25 Statue of
Evangeline,
St. Martinville

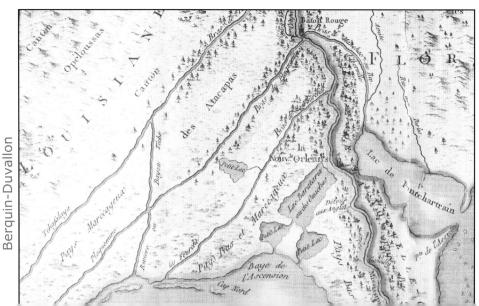

2.23 Cattle brands

Did you know...

On April 4, 1765, in New Orleans, eight Acadian men signed a contract for the raising of cattle with Antoine Dauterive of the Attakapas Post. This was the beginning of cattle farming in Louisiana. In 1773, Armand and Pierre Broussard, the sons of Beausoleil, began a regular cattle drive to New Orleans. After a few years, they were delivering over 150 head per month to the city.

When the Beausoleil Acadians arrived in Louisiana, the colony was officially Spanish, but actually in the hands of a caretaker French government. Moved by pity at the plight of the Acadian refugees, the French authorities provided the Acadians with what resources were available. Each family received seed grain, a shotgun, crude implements, and a land grant. Military engineer Louis Andry led them via the Mississippi and Bayou Plaquemine west to the Attakapas District. Other Acadians would arrive that year, most of them heading west, but a number settled at Cabannocé on the Mississippi above New Orleans in a region known as la Côte Acadienne. Through persistent hard work, the Acadians built productive farms. By 1767, numerous letters of invitation

2.24 Lower Louisiana in 1802

Berquin-Duvallon

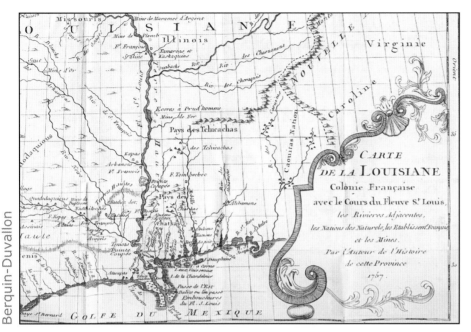

Berquin-Duvallon

2.26 Louisiana, 1767

CALL TO ACTION

Read "Evangeline" by Henry Wadsworth Longfellow. Using the poem as a basis, work with your classmates to write a dialogue between Evangeline and Gabriel in three parts:

1. Before the Deportation,

2. During the Deportation,

3. In exile with the two characters communicating at a distance.

Create a play using the dialogue and present the play to your school.

from Attakapas Acadians were circulating among their exiled relatives, particularly in Maryland and Pennsylvania. Pooling their meager resources to charter vessels to take them to Louisiana, many of the Acadians remaining in these colonies left Chesapeake Bay ports. They were frustrated, however, in their desire to settle near their kinsmen by the policy of the Spanish governor who intended to place the immigrants in strategic areas to thwart eventual British incursion from the east.

McNeese St.

2.27 Tilling the fields

Did you know...

The leaders of the Creole Revolt of 1768 enlisted the aid of Acadians living on the Côte Acadienne (Acadian Coast) north of New Orleans. Armed and led by the Creoles, approximately 200 Acadian men descended on the city and arrived at the residence of the Spanish governor, Ulloa. They escorted him by force to a ship anchored in the river. He was given three days to leave the colony, which he did on November 1.

Spanish Governor Ulloa was counting on the Acadians' military prowess and their hatred of the British to secure the frontier of the colony. In July 1767, 210 Acadians were assigned to Fort Saint Gabriel, and in February 1768, 149 of them were sent to San Luis de Natchez up the Mississippi River. This created great resentment among the Acadians.

They became active participants in the Creole Revolt of 1768, scores of Acadians descending on New Orleans to aid in chasing the Spanish governor from the colony.

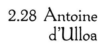

2.28 Antoine d'Ulloa

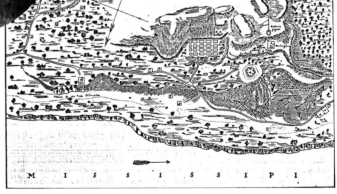

Antoine Declerck

2.29 The fort of San Luis de Natchez

Thirty years after the Deportation, the Acadian community of France was living in misery. After enduring several disastrous resettlement programs, the majority of the exiles were clustered around the ports of Western France, particularly Nantes and Saint Malo. Through a steady flow of correspondence, the exiles were aware of the successful Acadian settlement in Louisiana. In 1764, Henri Peyroux de la Coudrenière, a French soldier of fortune, visited the Acadian community in Louisiana. Learning that the Spanish government was actively seeking colonists, he devised a scheme to promote Acadian immigration to Louisiana, expecting a generous reward from the Spanish monarch.

CALL TO ACTION

Imagine that you are living on the Côte Acadienne and that you will participate in the Insurrection of 1768. Describe the trip to New Orleans, what you see and what you hear. Indicate on a map the exact route that you will take. Describe the method of transportation and the difficulties of the journey. Research the Acadian Coast today and accompany your text with images.

Gerard Braud

2.30 Saint-Malo

Gerard Braud

2.31 Nantes, 1785

© Robert Dafford

2.32 Acadians embarking at Nantes

Enlisting the aide of Acadian shoemaker Olivier Terrio, Peyroux was able, after years of negotiation, to overcome the skepticism of the Acadians and the resistance of the French government. Between May and October 1785, 1,596 Acadians, nearly the entire population residing in France, immigrated en masse aboard seven merchant vessels bound for New Orleans. Most of them settled along the banks of Bayou Lafourche. This was the greatest migration of Acadians into Louisiana and would be the final chapter of the exile of the Acadian community.

La Flottille de Nantes

Le Bon Papa   *La Ville d'Arcangel*

La Bergère   *La Caroline*

Le Beaumont   *L'Amitié*

Le Saint-Rémy

**THE SEVEN SHIPS THAT DEPARTED FOR
LOUISIANA FROM MAY TO OCTOBER, 1785**

CALL TO ACTION

Using a current map of Louisiana, show the areas which have settlements of Acadian descent. Explain why the descendants of the Acadians are living in these areas and explain why the original Acadians settled there.

NEW DISCOVERIES

Choose a theme from this chapter. List the discoveries that you made thanks to this chapter. Based on this list, create an exhibit of your discoveries using drawings and photos and display it in your classroom. Ask the permission of your school librarian to display it in the library. Create a program for your school radio station or a web-cast to explain your findings.

Chapter 3

The establishment of Acadian society *in Louisiana*

Louisiana

N
W   E
S

Mississippi River

Opelousas
Post

Bayou Teche

Attakapas
Post

New Orleans

Bayou Lafourche

Louisiana, circa 1765

0   100 km

© Elemore Morgan

3.1 Bayou dwelling

Acadian settlement in Louisiana fell into two basic patterns: watercourse strips and prairie hamlets. Strip villages were located along the Mississippi River, Bayou Lafourche, and Bayou Teche as well as smaller bayous and rivers. Acadians living in strip settlements communicated and traveled mostly by water in pirogues, flat-bottomed rowboats known as *bateau*, and small sailboats. Later, when roads were built along the crests of the natural levees, horse-drawn vehicles were used for transportation.

IMPORTANT DATES: FROM 1765 TO 1885

1765
The first Acadians arrive in Louisiana.

1768
Acadians take part in the Creole Revolt.

1785
The Flottille de Nantes transports 1,596 Acadians from France.

1803
French emperor Napoléon I sells Louisiana to the United States.

1804
The government of the Territory of Orleans is organized. William C.C. Claiborne is named governor.

1812
Louisiana becomes the 18th state of the United States.

The prairie

Prairie grasslands cover a large part of southwestern Louisiana. The prairies are bounded by forest growth that runs along the major streams. Between the larger rivers and bayous run smaller watercourses called *coulées*. The prairie is interspersed by ponds called *platins* or *marais* which collect water seasonally and may support a stand of trees. Underneath the topsoil is a claypan that is largely impermeable. On the prairies, as along the bayous, the primary original method of transportation in the Acadian settlements was by water.

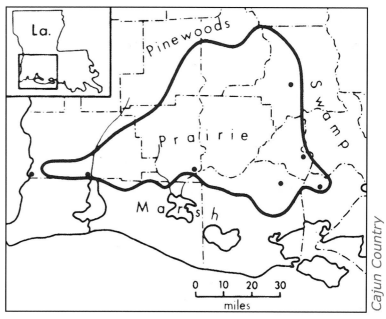

Cajun Country

3.2 The prairies of southwest Louisiana

1842	1861	1864	1865	1884	1885
A planter of Acadian heritage, Alexandre Mouton, is elected governor.	The Civil War begins.	Confederate General Alfred Mouton is killed at the Battle of Mansfield.	Civil War ends. Louisiana is occupied by Federal troops during Reconstruction.	The railroad arrives on the prairie of southwestern Louisiana.	Death of Alexandre Mouton.

CLS

3.3 Acadian weaver

 ettlement

Life on the prairies of southwest Louisiana in the nineteenth century was considerably different from that along the main rivers and bayous. North and west of the early settlements at Opelousas and Attakapas (St. Martinville) the prairie extends to the pine-covered hills of central Louisiana. Settlement density was low and concentrated in places known as *anses*. Prairie settlers were far more self sufficient than their counterparts who lived along the rivers. Most of the necessities of daily life were produced on the farmstead, including cloth that was hand-woven on upright looms.

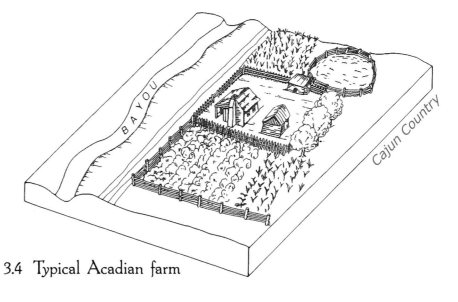

3.4 Typical Acadian farm

The marshes

The most distinctive and, to the original Acadian settlers, alien area of Louisiana was the coastal plain and marsh. The climate, vegetation, and fauna combined to produce an environment dramatically unlike anything the Acadians had ever seen. Yet, so completely did the Acadian immigrants adapt to this unique world, that today it represents, more than any other region, the distinctive culture of the Cajuns.

3.5 The Attakapas prairie

NEW DISCOVERIES

Using information found in this book and from your library or online, prepare a comparative table of the natural resources of southwest Louisiana. Illustrate the differences in the exploitation of resources in the early days of Acadian settlement and today.

© Kristie Cornell

rchitecture

Most of the Acadians who arrived in Louisiana between 1765 and 1795 built very simple homes. These were made of posts covered with thatch created from palmetto fronds in the manner of the Houma Indians. After a few years, a new style of house appeared. Constructed of ***poteaux en terre*** (post in ground) or ***planche debout*** (standing planks), these houses had floors of beaten earth. The next generation of Acadian house was more stable, with on-ground or raised posts, supported by cypress pillars. Mortar was applied between the posts and the beams, and ***bousillage***, a mixture of mud and Spanish moss, filled the space between the posts.

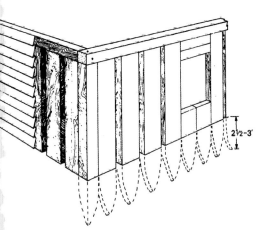
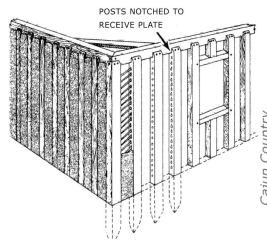

POSTS NOTCHED TO
RECEIVE PLATE

2½-3'

Cajun Country

3.6 Construction of *planche debout et poteaux en terre*

Did you know...

The basic form of the Acadian house remained the same throughout the nineteenth century. The typical house of the *petit habitant* (small farmer) was a raised rectangular structure. The attic, accessible by stairs from the front porch, was the bedroom of the adolescent boys, thus the name *garçonnière*. Otherwise the house was of a single room furnished with a buffet, a table, several chairs, an armoire, and several beds made by hand of cypress. There might also have been folding beds.

Louisiana Comprehensive Curriculum

UNIT 1:
Louisiana's Physical and Cultural Geography

ACTIVITY 5:
Louisiana's Personality: Regional

La chasse et la pêche

The swamps and marshes support an abundance of animal and aquatic life, which the early settlers quickly learned to identify and capture. Fur bearing animals, such as beaver, mink, otter, muskrat, raccoon, and bear were and are still trapped. Oysters, shrimp, crabs, and an abundance of fish supplied a rich and varied source of seafood. By the beginning of the nineteenth century, shellfish were shipped to New Orleans daily. Abundant waterfowl were hunted, as were alligators, turtles, frogs, and crawfish. Crawfish acquaculture began in the 1960s.

YOUR POINT OF VIEW

Why do you think the original Acadian families settled near water? Study a map of Louisiana to see if the Acadiana communities of today remain near a waterway. How do you think this proximity to water influenced the daily lives of the Acadians? Compare the situation of the original Acadians and their descendants today.

CLS

3.7 Trapper with skins

etits habitants

The nineteenth century was a period of great transformation in the Acadian society of Louisiana. The great majority of Acadians—known as *petits habitants*—were not materialistic in the modern sense, producing little beyond the necessities required to maintain the comfort of their families. They continued to perpetuate a traditional lifestyle in the relative isolation of the Lafourche Basin or in the open prairies of the southwest. Other Acadians, however, aspired to the social position and wealth of the planter aristocracy. The cohesive Acadian community fragmented as second and third-generation Acadians acquired slaves and embraced the values of the plantation system.

© Benny Graeff

3.8 The farm of a petit habitant

The planters

The transformation of Acadian society in the mid-nineteenth century is reflected by the growth in the number of slaves on Acadian owned plantations. The economic and cultural gap between the plantation owner and the typical Acadian farmer or petit habitant became greater and greater in the build-up to the Civil War. Wealth and economic power was concentrated more and more in the hands of the Acadian planter class, which came to define itself as "Créole." The term Acadian or Cajun came to be considered degrading.

Stephen Edwins

3.9 Plantation home

CALL TO ACTION

Visit a plantation home in person if possible or if not, on the internet. Imagine the daily life of the plantation owners. Visit the slave quarters. Imagine the daily lives of the slaves. Write a report that examines the contrast in lifestyle based on your discoveries.

3.10 Slave cabins

CLS

Louisiana Comprehensive Curriculum

UNIT 6:
The Early American Era of Louisiana

ACTIVITY 6:
Plantation Economy
P. 84-85 BLM
Market economy,
Flow Chart
(GLE #31, 48, 51, 62)

3.11 Alexandre Mouton

Alexandre Mouton was born in what is today Lafayette Parish. His father, Jean, was born in Acadie the year of the Deportation, 1755, and arrived in Louisiana as a very young child. Alexandre Mouton was elected governor of Louisiana in 1842. He supported the elimination of property qualifications for suffrage, according the vote to all free men. This insured him the support of the yeoman farmers. He was, nonetheless, a planter and the owner of 120 slaves. He presided over the Secession Convention of 1861 at which Louisiana declared its independence from the United States.

ar

Acadian society in the late antebellum period was divided into two ideological groups: staunchly pro-Southern rights planters and the far more numerous yeoman farmers who had little interest in the secessionist cause. In spite of these differences, the insular Acadians accepted the political leadership of the social elite and had great confidence in former U.S. senator and governor of Louisiana, Alexandre Mouton. On January 26, 1861, Mouton presided over the Louisiana secessionist convention in Baton Rouge that, by a vote of 113 to 17, dissolved the "union between the State of Louisiana and other States." The entire Acadian community, slaveholding or petit habitant, rich or poor, was dragged into a bitter sectional conflict that would forever change the social, political, and cultural life of Louisiana.

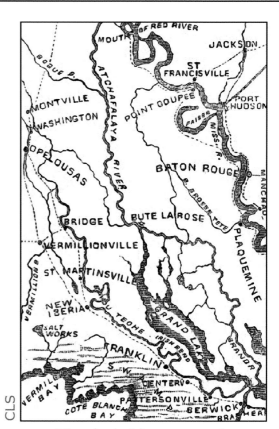

3.12 The Atchafalaya region during the Civil War

CLS

3.13 The Lafayette Parish courthouse during the Civil War

■ Acadiana during the Civil War

Confederate General Alfred Mouton, son of Alexandre, waged
a successful recruiting campaign among the prairie Acadians
in late 1861. However, most of the Acadian community
remained apathetic to the war. This indifference turned to
outright hostility following the enactment of the Confederate
Conscription Act. With the fall of New Orleans to the U.S.
Army in April 1862, the capital of Louisiana was moved
to Opelousas, in the very heart of the Acadian country. In
January 1863, Union General Nathaniel Banks launched a
full scale invasion of south-central Louisiana. Whether they
favored the war or not, the Acadians found themselves right in
the middle of it.

**Louisiana
Comprehensive
Curriculum**

UNIT 7:
Civil War and Reconstruction

ACTIVITY 1:
Louisiana Civil War Timeline
of Cause and Effects
P. 92-93, Political Differences
1 & 2 BLM
(GLE #62, 77)

CLS

3.14 Alfred Mouton

During the Battle of
Mansfield, April 8, 1864,
the 18th Louisiana Brigade
under the command of
General Jean-Jacques
Alfred Mouton, was placed
in the vanguard of the
Confederate forces. On
horseback and in plain
view, Mouton presented
a very visible target.
He was struck by a
Union sharpshooter.
Overcome with emotion
upon seeing their leader
mortally wounded,
the mostly Acadian
soldiers of his brigade
charged the federal
line. Under a blistering
fire from the Yankees,
the 18th Louisiana lost
more than one third of
its men.

CLS

■ Acadiana invaded

During the war, the communities of the Acadian prairie
of southwestern Louisiana were threatened not only by
Confederate conscription parties but also by paramilitary
bands of Jayhawkers. Acadian men fleeing conscription
were able to find refuge in the areas controlled by the
Jayhawkers, but these bands posed a serious threat to Acadian
farmsteads with their sporadic raids. The greatest threat,
however, was posed by General Banks's 40,000 man Union
army, which advanced toward Opelousas in September 1863.
Indiscriminate looting of civilian residences was common, the
federal troops taking horses, cattle, farm animals, and even
wooden fencing, leaving little in their wake.

3.15 The Battle of Prairie Carencro, November 3, 1863

CLS

3.16 Union soldiers foraging

◼ Reconstruction

The destruction of their farmsteads and the collapse of the
social order were the most visible manifestations of the new
and difficult circumstances in which Louisiana's Acadians
found themselves at the war's end. Roads which had been
poorly maintained even in the best of times were completely
neglected. Bridges were destroyed. The waterways were filled
with scuttled vessels rendering navigation impossible. The
Civil War left behind an enduring economic recession in the
Acadian parishes virtually without respite beginning in 1865.
Thousands of Confederate veterans, deserters, Jayhawkers,
camp followers, and newly freed slaves returned to their
homes. Most were incapable of supporting themselves,
stressing the very meager resources of the region.

CALL TO ACTION

Trace the route of the
invading Union army in
1863 from New Orleans
to north Louisiana. Count
the waterways using a
modern map and calculate
the number of bridges.
Imagine the life of the
civilian population along the
invasion route and write a
report on living in a war zone.
Are there civilian populations
who are suffering through
similar situations today? How
do their hardships compare
with those in Acadiana in 1863?
What are the differences? What
are the similarities?

**Louisiana
Comprehensive
Curriculum**

UNIT 7:
Civil War and Reconstruction

ACTIVITY 7:
Civil War Trading Cards
P. 95 (GLE #63, 73)

LOC

3.17 Cajun women washing clothes. This image was considered shocking at the time, illustrating Cajun women in degrading positions.

In 1873, lithographer A.R. Waud wrote: "These primitive people are the descendants of Canadian French settlers in Louisiana; and by the dint of intermarriage they have succeeded in getting pretty well down the social scale. Without energy, education, or ambition, they are good representatives of the white trash, behind the age in every thing."

■ Cajuns scorned

The declining economic fortunes of the "Cajuns," as Anglos called them, following the Civil War accelerated the process of social and cultural assimilation. The prestige of the Anglo-American elite became the benchmark of social success and those Cajuns who were able to afford to send their children to university preferred Anglo-American institutions. The culture and language of the Acadian subsistence farmers and laborers, sole heirs of their ethnic identity, became objects of derision.

3.18 Cajun family praying before a meal

© R. Roy

LOC

3.19 Musicians, 1927

YOUR POINT OF VIEW

What do you think of the comments of A.R. Waud? Do you think he took the trouble to try to understand the Cajuns or was he seeing them through his own prejudice? What do you think this quotation indicates about the perception of the Cajuns by the Anglo-Americans? Can you find another group that was treated in the same way? Do you think that mentalities have changed much since the time of A.R. Waud in the way that people generally see others?

NEW DISCOVERIES

Ask an elderly person to describe popular events in his or her day: dances, weddings, holidays, etc. Compare their accounts with the way in which these events are celebrated today. Which aspects of these popular celebrations have changed, and which have remained the same?

Cajun culture preserved

During the early settlement of the great southern triangle of Louisiana known today as Acadiana, there were few formal social institutions. Informal social groups were prevalent in isolated areas. Several distinctive social practices contributed to the evolution of Acadian society in Louisiana. Through collective events such as *boucheries*, *coups de main*, *bals de maison*, and *veillées*, the Acadian traditions of solidarity and inter-community aid were preserved. These traditions contributed to the preservation of a unique ethnic identity. Even as assimilation into the Anglo-American mainstream became more and more prevalent, traditional cultural expressions allowed the Acadians, or Cajuns, to maintain a unique identity.

Did you know...

As the Anglo-American culture began to dominate the social landscape of southwestern Louisiana, Acadian identity was transformed. Following the Civil War, Acadians increasingly intermarried outside of their community, absorbing people of German, English, Irish, and Spanish heritage into the group. No longer defined by strictly Acadian heritage, "Cajun" came to mean an ethnic group attached to the French language and a way of life.

LOC

3.20 Playing cards

■ The confrontation of cultures

Cajuns were noted for their hospitality, but although they welcomed strangers into their homes, most Cajuns resisted the materialistic values that they associated with Anglo-American society. Alcée Fortier, a prominent turn-of-the-century Louisiana historian, noted that the Acadians were "laborious, but they appear satisfied, if by cultivating their patch of ground with their sons, they manage to live with a little comfort." This notion was misunderstood by the Anglos who simply considered the Cajuns to be brutish and lazy.

3.21 Washing dishes

© Elemore Morgan Sr.

3.22 In the field

The great majority
of prairie Cajuns
were small farmers.
Plowing, planting,
hoeing, and
mending fences

3.23 Husking rice

filled the spring and early summer days. Early fall provided the
opportunity to hunt and fish. Cool weather signaled the harvest
season. The harvest was a communal undertaking in which all
of the members of the extended family participated. In spite
of the serious nature of the task and the hard work involved,
ramasseries often took on a festive atmosphere. Large quantities
of *gateaux de sirop*, coffee, and whiskey provided by the host
family punctuated the monotony of the work with shouts of joy,
songs, and animated talk.

YOUR POINT OF VIEW

Confronted with Anglo-
American cultural assimilation
and the imposition of the English
language in Louisiana, the
Cajuns adopted a non-conflictual
policy. Economic, political, and
social power were in the hands
of the Anglo-American elite,
and in the face of this reality,
the Cajuns submitted. Have you
ever experienced a situation in
which you were obliged to do
something that made you feel ill
at ease, something that you did
not approve of? Did you attempt
to resist? Or did you adopt a non-
conflictual policy? How did you
feel? What was the reaction of
your friends?

**Louisiana
Comprehensive
Curriculum**

UNIT 2:
Economic in Louisiana

ACTIVITY 6:
Four Basic Economic Questions
P. 25-26 (GLE #49)

■ Cattle farming

Cattle farming has been an important activity in Acadian culture from its very beginning in Louisiana. The Attakapas prairie is a natural pasture and perfectly suited for cattle. From the very first days of the settlement, Acadians supplied the city of New Orleans with beef. In the nineteenth century, the trip from the prairie to the city took about two weeks. Cattle farming is still an important element of life in southwest Louisiana, the seasons marked by herding, branding, and driving cattle.

3.24 Cowboys on the bridge over the Intracoastal Canal at l'Île Fourchue (Forked Island)

© Philip Gould

Did you know...

Each autumn, the cattle on the Attakapas prairie are herded to the marshes where the grass is abundant and stays green all winter. In the spring, before the mosquitoes become too aggressive, the cattle are assembled and branded. From there, they are herded north onto the prairie where they will spend the summer.

"It would take us a week to bring them in. We would drive them at night by the light of the moon, when the water was high."

– George Broussard

© Philip Gould

3.25 Carencro Raceways

▇ Les courses de chevaux

One aspect of rural life on
the Cajun prairie remains
unchanged: horse racing. A
strong tradition of horse racing
developed amongst the Cajun
cowboys. Sulky racing was
very popular until the 1960s,

© Philip Gould

3.26 A young jockey gets ready

and although harness racing has disappeared, quarter mile
races on a straight track are still very popular. Several Cajun
jockeys have enjoyed successful careers nationally, riding
throughout the United States.

NEW DISCOVERIES

In horse racing circles in the
United States, Louisiana is
known for its jockeys, amongst
the best in the country. Do a
search on the winner of the
Kentucky Derby over the last
ten years and count the number
of jockeys from Louisiana
(hint: Calvin Borel). On a map
of Louisiana, mark the home
towns of these jockeys. Can
you draw a conclusion from
this research? In which region
of Louisiana does horse racing
seem to be most popular? On
the same map mark the site of
all of the horse tracks that you
can find.

In 1884, Maurice Brien, originally from the Midwest, used a mechanical harvester to bring in his rice crop. Brien, who lived near Jennings, perfected his machine in 1886. Overnight this technological change dramatically increased the production of rice on the prairie. News of this increase spread rapidly, provoking a constant stream of immigration into southwest Louisiana in the last decades of the nineteenth century. In 1880 the population of the region was 126,067. In 1900 the population was 236,399, an increase of 90% due almost entirely to the success of commercial rice growing.

■ Rice growing

In the years following the Civil War, rice was grown on the prairies of southwest Louisiana. Thanks to a nearly impermeable claypan that lies about three feet below the surface, rice growing became an integral part of the local economy. Early rice farming was based on the "providence" method: levees were dug to collect rainwater and rice was planted within the levees. In 1894 a system of canals was dug near Jennings, permitting the flooding of the fields. Thanks to powerful pumps, water was drawn from the bayous into the canals and from the canals into the fields. This made large scale commercial rice farming possible.

© Kristie Cornell

3.27 Rice field

■ Shrimp fishing

Along Bayous Lafourche and Terrebonne, the principal economic activity is shrimp fishing. Shrimp boats are tied all along the bayous awaiting the opening of shrimp season when they will head out into the Gulf of Mexico.

The largest concentration of shrimpers is along Bayou Lafourche, but there are shrimping communities all along the Gulf Coast: from Saint Bernard and Plaquemines Parishes in the east, through Terrebonne Bay, Delcambre and Erath in Vermilion Parish, and as far as Cameron Parish and the boundary with Texas.

3.28 Fisherman and his shrimp

3.29 Shrimp boat, Bayou Lafourche

NEW DISCOVERIES

Make a list of Louisiana dishes that are based on seafood and rice. Search for similar dishes in other countries, particularly in French speaking countries (Haïti, Sénégal, Vietnam, etc.). Do the dishes in these countries contain the same ingredients as those found in Louisiana? Make a cookbook containing the recipes that you find.

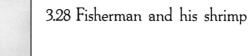

■ La cuisine cadienne

3.30 The basic ingredients
in Cajun cuisine

It is for good reason that Cajun cuisine has become a metaphor for the general culture. Like music, the French language, and Cajun architecture, the cuisine is a mix of several influences: Acadian, Spanish, German, American, Afro-Caribbean, and Native American. The heaviest influence, however, is French. Cajun cuisine is based on marinades, spices, and slow cooking in covered pots. The use of tomatoes and hot peppers comes from Spanish and Afro-Caribbean cooking. Gumbo, the most widely known dish, resembles a soup and is of African origin. The principal ingredient in gumbo is okra, which arrived in Louisiana from West Africa as a result of the slave trade. A second version of gumbo is made from roux, a thick paste made from cooking flour in oil. Roux is French in origin. *Filé*, made from ground up sassafras leaves,

3.31 Crawfish étouffée

is derived from the Native Americans and is used to thicken the sauce.

© Kristie Cornell

© Conni Castille/Mary Tutweiller

■ Crawfish

Nothing symbolizes Cajun cuisine more than crawfish. This little fresh water crustacean was not available commercially until the 1960s. Before then, crawfish were caught and consumed in the home.

3.32 Crawfish

CALL TO ACTION

With your classmates, collect several Louisiana recipes. With the recipes, prepare a cookbook with illustrations. Design the cover to include the name of your school and of your class. Print several copies, which you can offer for sale or give as gifts on behalf of your class.

After commercial crops became available, restaurant chefs—and domestic chefs as well—began to experiment with cooking the tails in sauce.

Crawfish étouffée is the king of Cajun dishes. Originally this dish was called a "courtbouillon." In the 1920s it was served at the Hébert Hotel in Breaux Bridge, prepared by the Hébert sisters, Yolie and Marie. Around 1940 they gave the recipe to Aline Guidry Champagne, owner of the Rendez-Vous Restaurant. One day a client happened to ask Mrs. Champange what she was cooking. "J'apè étouffer des écrevisses," she responded, "I am smothering some crawfish." And that is how the dish got its name.

This dish has done more than any other to popularize Cajun cuisine. The recipe enjoyed a prominent place in all of the early Cajun cookbooks published in the 1950s. From that time on most Cajun restaurants have served it.

There is a specific storytelling tradition in Mamou called "les histoires de Pascal." These stories are not fixed but are improvised in a conversational style. Based on exaggeration, lies, and absurd details, these stories relate the adventures of a certain Pascal. The storytellers meet one another in the bars along Sixth Street, particularly Fred's Lounge. They then launch into the stories, improvising in the most informal fashion during card games or other group activities.

◼ Storytelling

A rich and varied storytelling tradition is part of the Cajun culture of Louisiana. The stories can be animal fables or stories of kings and castles. The arrival of television and the dominance of the English language has relegated this tradition to the margins of Cajun society. Nonetheless, tall tales can erupt spontaneously in barber shops, bars, on the steps of church, at service stations, at funeral homes, just about anywhere that people gather.

© Philip Gould

3.33 On a street in Mamou

Jean Sot à l'école

Clotile Richard, Carencro

Jean Sot avait été à l'école pour apprendre l'anglais. Ça fait, il a revenu back pour visiter son père et sa mère, et il faisait comme s'il comprenait plus le français.

Ça fait, il a été au jardin (son père et sa mère faisaient jardin) pour visiter. Et puis, il voit les rateaux et la pioche. Ça fait, il voulait demander à sa mère ce que c'était cet outil, pour travailler le jardin. Et puis, en même temps, il met son pied sur le rateau. Le rateau a revenu back, l'a frappé sur la bouche. "Ah!" il dit. "Mon sacré tonnerre de rateau!"

"Ah," elle dit, "mon garçon, je vois ton français commence à te revenir!"

NEW DISCOVERIES

A project for a small group: Consult *Cajun and Creole Folktales* (Ancelet, University Press of Mississippi, 1994) and pick a story. Illustrate the story. Visit an elementary class and read the story to the students. Record the story and make it available to all of the classes in your school.

Jean Sot at School

Clotile Richard, Carencro

Jean Sot had gone to school and was obliged to learn English. When he came back home and saw his father and mother, he acted as though he no longer understood French.

He went into the garden where his father and mother were working. He saw a rake and a hoe. Pretending not to know what they were, he asked his mother speaking English, "What are these?" At the same time, he put his foot down on the rake. The rake came back and hit him on the mouth. "Oh!" he exclaimed, "Mon sacré tonnerre de rateau!" (you damn thunderation of a rake)

"Ah, my son!" she said, "I see your French is coming back to you!"

NEW DISCOVERIES

Louisiana French stories often are based on the fabulous and the imaginary. With your classmates, write a story in the spirit of a folk tale with a Louisiana animal as the primary character. Take turns creating the story, each of you writing a few lines. Try to imagine adventures based on natural challenges, such as a hurricane. Once you have finished the story, illustrate the story with drawings and present it to your class. Publish the illustrated story in your school newspaper.

Did you know...

A *traiteur* (healer) learns his or her practice from another traiteur. Most often this folk knowledge will be passed from a family member of an older generation to a younger relative of the opposite sex. Each traiteur possesses a repertoire of prayers for particular maladies and the rituals performed are adapted in a very personal style. Generally traiteurs do not accept payment for their services.

Delmay Guillory

3.34 Prie-Dieu

■ Les traiteurs

Many Cajuns continue to practice some form of folk medicine, especially in the rural areas. This practice evolved through the confluence of three traditions that shared a similar world vision: the Acadian tradition brought from Acadie, the Afro-Louisiana tradition, and the Native American tradition. **Traiteurs** or healers still practice in southwest Louisiana. Their practice is both mystical and practical. Catholic prayers, candles, and rosary beads are used. In addition, a traiteur should have a knowledge of medicinal herbs. Homeopathic medicine, based on the use of plants, was very popular amongst the original Acadian settlers and much of that tradition has been preserved. Many such treatments resemble those found in Canada and France.

Vermilionville

3.35 Healing herbs

■ La religion Catholique

CLS

3.36 The blessing of the fleet

The Catholic religion is dominant in Cajun society and its rituals are present at life's significant events: birth, marriage, and death. Cajun culture also contains many para-religious traditions. Each year, a Catholic priest will bless the sugarcane fields near New Iberia and Jeanerette. In the towns along the coast such as Delcambre, the shrimp fleet is blessed by the local priest at the beginning of the season. Eating seafood on Friday and during Lent is a common practice. Without a doubt, the most unique event of the Catholic calendar in southwest Louisiana is Mardi Gras.

NEW DISCOVERIES

Prepare a list of Catholic feast days that are celebrated in southwest Louisiana. Describe the manner in which these feasts are celebrated. What is the influence of these practices on society in general in Louisiana?

NEW DISCOVERIES

Prepare a book containing home remedies and describing the traditional methods used to cure illness. Describe the plants used. Try to find a traiteur or someone who knows of a traiteur. Describe your impression of these practices.

La chanson des Mardis gras*

Les Mardis gras, ça vient de l'Angleterre,

Tout le tour, le tour du moyeu.

Ça passe une fois par an demander la charité

Quand même si c'est une tite poule maigre

Et trois ou quatre coton-maïs.

Les Mardis gras, c'est pas des malfaicteurs

C'est juste des quémandeurs.

Capitaine Sosthène demande

Ouais, au maître et la maîtresse

La permission de rentrer pour demander la charité.

Les Mardis gras sont sur un grand voyage,

Tout le tour, le tour du moyeu.

Ça passe une fois par an demander la charité,

Quand même si c'est une patate,

Une patate et des *gratons.*

*translation - page 117

© Lucius Fontenot

3.37 Mardi Gras mask

■ Mardi Gras

Mardi Gras marks the beginning of Lent. The tradition of Mardi Gras has its roots in the European tradition of the celebration of spring. The Cajun carnival is derived from the *fête de la quémande* (feast of begging), which has been celebrated since the Middle Ages. Masked and costumed celebrants roamed the countryside offering a performance, a dance, or a song, in exchange for a gift. In the Cajun *Courir du Mardi Gras* (Mardi Gras Run), masked horsemen visit the farmsteads of the community. Arriving at a farm, the riders dance and sing for the farmer and his family in hopes of receiving a contribution for the communal gumbo to be served in the evening.

The costumes worn by the Mardi Gras riders are inspired by the dress of the Middle Ages and are meant to make fun of the elite. The pointed hats resemble those worn by the ladies of the court, and the mortar board hats mock those worn by professors. The courir is a form of organized anarchy in which the riders are allowed wild behavior but within a very well defined and tightly controlled context. The Capitaine is unmasked and exercises absolute control over the riders. No *coureur* can enter a farmstead without the Capitaine's permission. No coureur can be armed. The only alcohol available is that which is distributed by the Capitaine. No coureur can defy the Capitaine during the ride.

Arriving at a farmstead, the Capitaine waves a white flag and enters the property alone. He greets the farmer and asks permission to allow the coureurs to enter, pledging personal responsibility for their actions. Once the signal is given (waving of the flag), the coureurs arrive at a gallop. They will dismount to sing and dance in hopes of getting a contribution from the farmer. This can be flour, rice, potatoes, onions, or even money. The preferred gift is a live chicken that will be launched into the air and chased by the riders. This scene is repeated time and again during the day until the cortege returns to the village and the point of departure. A masked ball will go into the night, but precisely at the stroke of midnight, the party comes abruptly to a halt and Lent begins.

NEW DISCOVERIES

Do you celebrate Mardi Gras? Using photos, explain the experience of Mardi Gras. Compile a list of towns in south Louisiana that celebrate Mardi Gras. Compare the traditions of each locality. Why do you think Mardi Gras is so popular? Try to find other countries where Mardi Gras, or Carnival, is celebrated. Compare these traditions with the traditions found in Louisiana.

© Lucius Fontenot

3.38 Coureurs de Mardi Gras

CALL TO ACTION

Study the traditional Mardi Gras costumes of the Cajun prairie. Make several drawings of various costumes and collect them into a book. Using your drawings, make a Mardi Gras costume and mask.

Chapter 4

Contemporary Cajun society in *Louisiana*

© David Simpson

Michael Doucet

CODOFIL

Jimmie Domengeaux

© Lucius Fontenot

Oil Rig

© Lucius Fontenot

Rice Harvest

© Philip Gould

Festivals
Acadiens et Créoles

© Alyce Labry

Feufollet

CLS

4.1   Railroad at the beginning of the 20th century

The railroad arrived on the Cajun prairie of Louisiana in the 1880s. Although the area had enjoyed access to the outside world via the Bayous Vermillion and Teche and the Mermentau River, the railroad significantly reduced the isolation of Cajun society and introduced elements of American culture that would have a significant impact in rural south Louisiana. Travel to and from the city of New Orleans was greatly facilitated, allowing manufactured goods to flow into southwestern Louisiana much more readily than ever before. The railroad also allowed produce of the area, particularly rice, quicker access to market.

IMPORTANT DATES: FROM 1881 TO 1999

1881
The railroad arrives on the Cajun prairie.

1901
Oil is discovered in Jennings.

1916
Compulsory education law is adopted.

1921
The Constitution of Louisiana is modified to eliminate French from public affairs.

1927
The Acadian Miracle by Dudley LeBlanc is published.

1928
The first recording of Cajun music, "Allons à Lafayette" by Joe Falcon.

1955
Commemoration of the bicentennial of the Déportation of 1755.

French threatened

CLS

4.2 Students at Mire, early 20th century

The first decades of the twentieth century were difficult for the French language that was still spoken by the majority of Cajuns. According to the U.S. census of 1900, approximately 85% of the population of southwest Louisiana was French speaking. In 1916, the Louisiana legislature adopted a compulsory education law requiring all children above the age of six to attend school. The public schools were Anglophone institutions and were powerful forces of assimilation. The great majority of young Cajuns had no experience with the English language. They were humiliated and punished, often physically, when speaking French, their first language. The constitution of the State of Louisiana was revised in 1921, and the official status of the French language was eliminated.

NEW DISCOVERIES

Do a study amongst older Cajuns to find out their experiences at school. Ask them if they spoke French at school and how this was perceived. Try to determine how a typical school day was conducted in the 1930s and 1940s. Compare this with a typical day in your school.

YOUR POINT OF VIEW

On the internet, find French speaking organizations in Louisiana that address themselves to young students. Find French speaking organizations elsewhere who share the same focus.

1964
The Balfa Brothers play at the Newport Folk Festival.

1968
The Council for the Development of French in Louisiana (CODOFIL) is created.

1971
The Louisiana legislature creates a 22 Parish economic zone. United by its Acadian heritage, this area is called Acadiana.

1974
First Festivals Acadiens et Créoles in Lafayette.

1980
First French immersion class created in Lake Charles.

1996
Action Cadienne is founded.

1999
The Acadian World Congress is held in Louisiana.

Did you know...

During the Second World War, hundreds of young Cajun men volunteered to join the armed forces. Speaking French was a considerable military asset in Africa and Belgium as well as France. The French speaking Cajuns assisted in communicating with the French Resistance after D-Day. They likewise ensured communication with the French population giving important military information to the Allies.

World War II

World War II was a great force of assimilation among the Cajuns. Many of the able-bodied men between eighteen and thirty-five volunteered or were drafted into the military. Some of them had never before left their home parishes. The encounter with Anglo-American society would radically change the identity of a whole generation of Cajuns. To their parents, the "Américains" were English-speaking outsiders, but the identity of the young men of the generation that fought in World War II was both Cajun and American.

© Kristi Guillory

4.3 Young Cajuns in the U.S. Air Force

Oil—a force of assimilation

Oil was discovered in Jennings, Louisiana, in 1901. Beginning in the 1930s, the oil business became a major economic engine in southwest Louisiana. A worker could make as much money in a month in the oil patch as he could all year long as a farmer. Many Cajuns immigrated to east Texas to work in the oil refineries that offered good wages. Cajun families settled

4.4 Oil field worker

in Beaumont, Port Arthur, and Orange. In Louisiana, as in Texas, English was the language of the oil patch and a *Cadien* who hoped to work in the oil business was obliged to speak it.

© Elmore Morgan

4.5 Cajuns working on an oil rig

NEW DISCOVERIES

Research the economic crisis of the 1930s among people who lived though the period. Ask them how they survived the Great Depression. Try to find out especially if they have any memories of community assistance between Cajuns, black Creoles, and Native Americans. Write a report and present it to your class.

CALL TO ACTION

Prepare an illustrated calendar including photos and drawings dealing with the agricultural economy of Louisiana. Try to include activities from the 1930s, 1940s, and 1950s.

La musique cadienne

Of all aspects of Cajun culture, its music is certainly the most well known. Forged in the crucible of south Louisiana from American, Irish, German, Spanish, and Native American, as well as Acadian French elements, Cajun music has a rich and complex history. The violin, popular in France during the period of the original colonization of Acadie, was the main musical instrument of Acadian society before the Deportation of 1755. It was likewise the dominant instrument in south Louisiana in the years following the arrival of the Acadian exiles. This changed at the end of the nineteenth century, when local merchants began to import ten-button diatonic accordions from Germany.

The accordion style of Cajun music defines its character. Cadien and black Creole musicians adapted the instrument to the local dance culture near the end of the nineteenth century. In a process that recalls the creation of jazz and blues, a new style was created. This new music was simply called *la musique française* (French music).

© Zachary Richard

4.6 Fiddle and accordion

◼ The accordion

At the beginning of the twentieth century, ten-button diatonic accordions were imported into south Louisiana in great numbers. Built in Germany, these accordions were particularly prized by the Cajuns because of their durability. The two best known brands were Sterling and Monarch. Known as *petits noirs* (little black ones), because of their color, they had all but disappeared by the 1950s. In 1960, Marc Savoy of Eunice, began to build accordions. His work served as a model for many local accordion builders. At the beginning of the twenty-first century, dozens of builders are producing diatonic "Cajun" accordions.

4.7 Marc Savoy in his workshop

© Philip Gould

YOUR POINT OF VIEW

Do you think that the Festival International de Louisiane, the Zydeco Festival, and Festivals Acadiens et Créoles are important for the culture of southwest Louisiana? Explain your answer.

NEW DISCOVERIES

Consult an accordion builder and determine the stages and the materials necessary in the construction of a Cajun accordion. List all of the parts and explain the process. What are the necessary tools? Accompany your report with drawings to show the pieces and the way in which they are assembled.

CLS

4.8 Cléoma Breaux and
Joe Falcon

Cléoma Breaux had an enormous impact on Cajun music. She was able to reconcile a professional musical career with family life in an era when there was little place for women in the world of music. Her talent was immense and her voice absolutely unique. Her recordings had considerable success, but her greatest re-cognition came in the dance halls. Because she performed alongside her husband, Joe Falcon, she was able to thwart the criticism of those who believed that a woman had no place performing in the dance halls. Her career was ended tragically in 1940 by an automobile accident. She died a year later.

■ The first recordings

Commercial recording companies like Decca, Columbia, RCA Victor, and Bluebird began recording regional and ethnic music throughout America in the early twentieth century. In south Louisiana, French language 78 rpm recordings were sold along with the gramophones needed to play them. These recordings contributed to the renown of the musicians who made them and spread their influence throughout the region, thus creating a standard repertoire. The first Cajun recording was "Allons à Lafayette," released in 1928 by Joseph Falcon.

CLS   4.9 Amédé Ardoin

In the early days of the twentieth century, Cajun and black Creole musicians played together. Cajun fiddler Dennis McGee performed regularly with black Creole accordionist Amédé Ardoin. Together they created much of what was to become the core repertoire of Cajun music. Others like Leo Soileau, Mayus Lafleur, Moise Robin, the Walker Brothers, the Segura Brothers, and Angelas Lejeune were part of the first wave of recorded Cajun music, refining and defining the style in the process.

■ The String Band era

CLS

4.10 The Hackberry Ramblers

By the mid-1930s, Anglo-American influence, sustained by the oil business and the public schools, overwhelmed Cajun culture. Accordions began to fade from the scene with the arrival of more typical American styles. Western swing, country, and popular radio tunes made their way into the Cajun repertoire, although usually sung in French. String bands like the Hackberry Ramblers and Soileau's Four Aces were at the forefront of this musical assimilation. As the field recordings John and Alan Lomax captured between 1934 and 1937 prove, the older styles, including ballads whose origins date back to western France, were still nonetheless an important aspect of the musical culture of southern Louisiana.

NEW DISCOVERIES

Download recordings from southwest Louisiana from the 1920s, 1930s, 1940s, 1950s, and 1960s. For example: Joe Falcon (1920s), The Hackberry Ramblers (1930s), Iry LeJeune (1940s), Rod Bernard (1950s), and the Balfa Brothers (1960s), or other artists of your choice. Compare the recordings. Note the similarities; note the differences. Compare the instrumentation and the styles. Analyze the evolution of the culture in general in light of the evolution of the music.

CLS

4.11 Iry LeJeune

Iry LeJeune was born on October 28, 1928, near Pointe Noire. Legally blind, he devoted himself to playing the accordion. Before he turned twenty he was recognized as a tremendous musician. In 1948, accompanied by fiddle player Floyd LeBlanc, Iry traveled to Houston to record "La valse du pont d'amour" ("The Love Bridge Waltz") for Opera Records. This recording was immensely popular and was a turning point for Cajun music. At the height of his popularity, Iry LeJeune died tragically in an automobile accident. He was twenty-six years old.

■ Post-WWII

LOC/CLS

4.12 Dancehall in the 1940s

WWII was a watershed event for Cajun culture and for Cajun music as well. Upon returning home many Cajun G.I.s immersed themselves in their French language culture and were regular customers at the local dancehalls. In contrast to the house dances popular before the war, the commercial dancehalls became the focus of Cajun music. Trap drum kits, pedal steel guitars, and amplification were ubiquitous and permitted bands to play in larger venues. In 1948, a nearly blind accordion player from the heart of the Cajun prairie released a 78 rpm recording called "La valse du pont d'amour." The song transformed Cajun music forever and made its creator, Iry Lejeune, the most influential Cajun musician of all time.

Propelled by ever increasing popularity of the post-WWII electrified Cajun style, a host of bands created regular employment for a cadre of professional musicians. Austin Pitre, Lawrence Walker, Aldus Roger, Belton Richard, Walter Mouton, Octa Clark, Hector Duhon, Blackie Forestier, Alphé and Shirley Bergeron, and Nathan Abshire were part of the dancehall phenomenon and could be found playing every weekend and often in between in the dozens of dancehalls that were found in practically every town in south Louisiana.

Swamp Pop

By the 1960s, Cajun music was in danger of being overwhelmed by popular American music. A new local style, called Swamp Pop, had evolved in the 1950s. Johnny Allen (Guillot), Warren Storm (Schexnayder), Rod Bernard, and Bobby Charles (Guidry) sang in English and performed in a style that had more in common with American rock and roll than accordion-based Cajun music. In spite of the declining fortunes of French language recordings, D.L. Menard's song "La porte en arrière," ("The Back Door") became a smash regional hit in 1960. It was, however, the last influential Cajun recording of the post-WWII period and marked the end of an era.

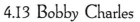

4.13 Bobby Charles

Bernard

CALL TO ACTION

Search the internet for Swamp Pop artists. Compare these Louisiana artists with American rock and roll artists of the same period. What are the similarities? What are the differences? Present your findings to your class.

Shane Bernard

4.14 Rod Bernard and the Twisters

4.15 Dewey Balfa

Dewey Balfa was born in March 1927 in Grand Louis, a small community west of Mamou in Evangeline Parish. Dewey learned his first songs from his grandmother. From his father he learned to play the violin. During WWII, he worked in Orange, Texas, at a naval yard. He returned to Louisiana in 1948 and began to play music professionally with his brothers Rodney and Will. In 1979, Dewey's two brothers were killed in a car accident. He continued to play, becoming an ambassador of Cajun music throughout the world.

Modern Cajun music

In 1964, Gladius Thibodeaux, Louis Vinesse Lejeune, and Dewey Balfa performed at the Newport Folk Festival. National organizations like Newport and the Smithsonian Institution had begun to encourage traditional Cajun music, sending folklorists and fieldworkers to record the old styles and identify the outstanding performers. The Newport Festival of 1964 was a watershed event. Dewey Balfa returned to Louisiana to contradict the naysayers who had predicted that he would be laughed off the stage at Newport. He wanted to, as he said, "let people in Louisiana hear the echo of the applause." Cajun music had entered the modern period.

CLS

4.16 Les frères Balfa

© Elemore Morgan

4.17 Zachary Richard and Michael Doucet at Festivals Acadiens, 1975

In the early 1970s, Cajun music remained the provision of older musicians. Amongst the first younger musicians to experiment with the style was Zachary Richard. His first recording contract with Electra Records in 1972 provided an occasion to acquire a diatonic Cajun accordion. Incorporating elements of contemporary American folk-rock music along with traditional Cajun themes, Richard and Michael Doucet toured France in 1973. The tour had a major impact on both of their careers. Zachary Richard would ultimately leave for Québec and begin a French language songwriting career. Michael Doucet would remain in Louisiana and form one of the most influential traditional Cajun bands of the modern era, Beausoleil.

© Stuart Brinin

4.18 Zachary Richard, 1980

NEW DISCOVERIES

Study the program of activities at the Festival International de Louisiane and Festivals Acadiens et Créoles. Do you think that the programming of these festivals caters to young music fans? Write a letter to the organizers of these festivals and suggest activities adapted to young students. Conceive the activities in order to promote the knowledge of Cajun music.

CALL TO ACTION

Write the biography of a Louisiana artist and publish it in your school newspaper. Send a copy to radio stations in south Louisiana (KBON, KRVS) and request that the biography be read on the air.

4.19 Sheryl Cormier

Cajun music is traditionally the domain of male musicians, but several women musicians have been successful and have contributed considerably to the musical culture of southwest Louisiana. Following in the footsteps of Cléoma Breaux, artists like Bonsoir Catin, The Magnolia Sisters, Sheryl Cormier, and Christine Balfa have carved a place for themselves. Inez Catalan and Marce Lacouture are ballad singers preserving a unique folk heritage. All have enriched Cajun music with a feminine point of view.

Post-modern Cajun music

Post-modern Cajun music is the most vibrant aspect of contemporary Cajun culture. Traditional styles still prevail but run the gamut from acoustic folk to hard driving dance music.

4.20 The Pine Leaf Boys

Wayne Toups, Bruce Daigrepont, Steve Riley, and David Greely each have a unique personal style and enjoy a devoted following. A new generation of young Cajun musicians is putting its own stamp on the tradition. The Lost Bayou Ramblers, Pine Leaf Boys, and Feufollet have brought a new perspective. Cedric Watson, a young black musician originally from Texas, explores the frontier between Cajun and Zydeco. Other musicians such as Paul Daigle, Johnny Sonnier, Terry Huval, and Eddie Lejeune continue to pay homage to the dance hall style of the 1950s. Resurrected like the phoenix from its nadir in the early 1960s, Cajun music in its various incarnations continues to inspire and bring joy to people not only in Louisiana but around the world.

The Arts

Poetry

In 1980, les Éditions Intermède in Montréal, Canada, published *Cris sur le bayou,* the first anthology of contemporary Louisiana French language poetry. Louisiana enjoyed a rich French literary tradition in the nineteenth century, but this was primarily an expression of the Creole society of New Orleans. Although French was the language of business in Acadian Louisiana into the twentieth century and the language of official documents in many Acadiana parishes, there had never been a specifically Acadian French language literature until this publication in 1980. Since that time, a number of Louisiana French authors, including Jean Arceneaux, David Cheramie, Debbie Clifton, Kirby Jambon, and Zachary Richard continue to publish in French, encouraged particularly by the Acadian publishing company Perce Neige in New Brunswick, Canada.

Chêne vert

Chêne vert,
Et noir,
Et fort,
Plein de glands
Qui tombent impuissants
En automne
Sur les nouveaux toits
Qui ont enhavi son ombrage,
Qui ont coupé ses racines
Pour faire leurs fondations
Qui ont tronqué ses branches
Pour faire de la place
Et pour embêter les écureuils
Qui se mêlent dans leurs courses
Après trois cents ans d'habitudes.

– Jean Arceneaux

Green Oak

Green oak,
And black,
And strong,
Filled with acorns,
That fall feebly
In the autumn
On the new roofs
That have invaded your shade,
That have cut your roots
To make their foundations
That have pruned your branches
To make room
And to annoy the squirrels
Whose habits are now confused
After the habits of three hundred years.

– Jean Arceneaux

4.21 *Crawfish Eater*, by Francis Pavy

4.22 *Jolie Blonde*, by George Rodrigue

4.23 *Back Porch Waltz*, by Floyd Sonnier

Fine Arts

4.24 *Louisiana Marsh*, by David Alpha

Although not specifically defined by Acadian heritage, there is an important school of painting that is associated with Cajun culture. The primary style is impressionist and the primary subject is landscape. The most recognized

© Philip Gould

4.25 Elemore Morgan Jr.

artist in the genre is Elemore Morgan Jr., whose work is largely inspired by the prairie. David Alpha works in a similar style. Melissa Bonin's work is atmospheric and often uses bayou waterways as inspiration. George Rodrigue is well known for his Cajun domestic scenes dominated by a dark image of the live oak. His "Blue Dog" paintings have gained him recognition worldwide. Francis Pavy works in a style that is nourished by the iconic images of south Louisiana that he transforms into powerfully evocative scenes. Floyd Sonnier created more traditional images of rural Cajun life.

■ Film

©Pitre, Mire, Larroque

4.26 Michelle Benoit and Glen Pitre / Pat Mire / Charles Larroque

Resisting the predilection to relocate to the traditional cinematographic capital of California, native filmmakers have produced films that are deeply tied to the Cajun experience. A native of Cutoff on Bayou Lafourche, Glen Pitre is best known for his feature-length film *Belizaire the Cajun* and has produced and directed numerous documentaries in partnership with his wife, Michelle Benoit.

Pat Mire is a native of the Cajun prairie. His work includes the feature length *Dirty Rice* and the award winning documentary *Against the Tide*. Charles Larroque, a native of Jeanerette, has produced several French language pieces dealing with Acadian culture including *Gumbo La La* and *Coeurs Batailleurs*.

CALL TO ACTION

Using a digital camera, make a short documentary film between 5 and 15 minutes long. The theme of the film should be "La vie cadienne" ("Cajun Life"). The film should illustrate what you believe to be the essence of Cajun life today. With your classmates, organize a film festival screening all of the films. Ask your school to organize a jury to select the best film.

■ Photography

Similar to the visual arts, there exists a school of photography associated with Cajun culture. The primary subject matters are the people, particularly the musicians, and the landscape of south Louisiana. Besides his work as a painter, Elemore Morgan Jr. is known for his photography. His collection *The Makers of Cajun Music* is a classic in the genre. Philip Gould has published numerous books including *Cajun Music and Zydeco, Louisiana Faces*, and *Les Cadiens d'Asteur*. Greg Girouard celebrates the natural environment of the Atchafalaya Basin. Although not directly associated with the Cajun tradition, Kent Hutslar is one of the most recognized photographers in Acadiana. His experiments with coloration create a unique and evocative universe.

4.27 *Fire in the Swamp*, by Greg Girouard

4.28 Greg Girouard

4.29 Philip Gould

4.30 Kent Hutslar

Academic studies

This book would not have been possible without the work of the historians of the Cajun community. Neglected by American historians, the history of the Cajun people of Louisiana has survived thanks to its own historians. In 1927 Dudley LeBlanc published *The Acadian Miracle,* a groundbreaking work. It was not until the 1970s, however, that the history of the Cajuns was studied rigorously. Foremost among the scholars is Carl Brasseaux. His works, *The Founding of New Acadia, Scattered to the Wind,* and *From Acadian to Cajun* are the basis of all subsequent study. A new generation of historians is continuing his work. Keith Fontenot, Ryan Brasseaux, and Shane Bernard are exploring new aspects of the Cajun story of the twentieth century. Barry Jean Ancelet has devoted his professional life to the study of Cajun culture. His numerous works examine and preserve Cajun musical and folk traditions.

4.31 Barry Jean Ancelet

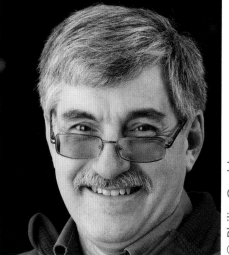

4.32 Carl Brasseaux

Les militants

In spite of the social pressure of Anglo-American assimilation, there were activists in southern Louisiana who resisted the tide of Americanization. At the forefront of the Acadian cultural movement was Dudley J. LeBlanc. His book, *The Acadian Miracle*, published in 1927, was a significant event in the preservation of the history of the Louisiana Acadians. The Acadian Bicentennial Celebration, held in 1955, was the occasion for a reaffirmation of Acadian identity. In 1968, CODOFIL (The Council for the Development of French in Louisiana) was founded by legislative decree. In the face of the relentless adverse pressure of assimilation, the French language and Acadian culture are still vital elements of the society of southern Louisiana.

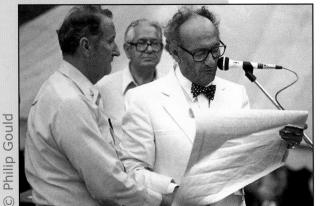

4.33 Dewey Balfa, Jimmie Domengeaux, Paul Tate

★ Dudley J. LeBlanc

4.34 Dudley J. LeBlanc

Born in Lafayette Parish on August 16, 1894, Dudley LeBlanc was raised in Abbeville. Elected a member of the Louisiana House of Representatives in 1924, he ran unsuccessfully for governor in 1932, but was elected state senator in 1940, 1948, 1964, and 1968. LeBlanc was a stalwart supporter of Acadian culture. His weekly radio show in French was hugely popular.

A successful businessman, LeBlanc's health tonic Hadacol made him a fortune. The Hadacol Caravan toured the United States featuring such celebrities as George Burns, Mickey Rooney, Milton Berle, Bob Hope, and Hank Williams Sr. LeBlanc was instrumental in the creation of the Council for the Development of French in Louisiana, CODOFIL. He passed away in 1971.

© Philip Gould

4.35 Jimmie Domengeaux

★ Jimmie Domengeaux

Born in Lafayette on January 6, 1907, James R. Domengeaux attended Southwestern Louisiana Institute and obtained his law degree from Tulane University in 1931. Elected to the Louisiana House of Representatives in 1940, he was subsequently elected to the U.S. House. In 1968, he was appointed as president of the Council for the Development of French in Louisiana. For his efforts to save the French language in Louisiana, Domengeaux received an honorary doctorate from Louisiana State University, the Order of the Legion of Honor from the French government, and the Order of the Crown of Belgium. In the 1980s, Domengeaux implemented a new and highly successful teaching method: French immersion.

YOUR POINT OF VIEW

In your area, can you find someone who speaks French in a restaurant, a store, or other public place? Can you find billboards or signs in French? Do you see any television ads in French? Do you think that the French language is important for Cajun culture? Do you think that the French language should be protected by law? Discuss with your classmates and with your family. Is it important to speak French? Explain your point of view.

Blanco

4.36 Kathleen Blanco

✳ Kathleen Blanco

Kathleen Babineaux Blanco was born December 15, 1942, in New Iberia. In 2003, she was elected the 54th governor of Louisiana, the first woman to hold the post. She took her oath of office on January 12, 2004, in French and English. Throughout her career, Kathleen Babineaux Blanco has promoted the links between Louisiana and the French speaking world.

✳ Warren Perrin

4.37 Warren Perrin

Perrin

Warren A. Perrin was president of CODOFIL from 1994 to 2010. He is the founder of the Acadian Museum in Erath. In 1990, Perrin launched the "Petition for an Apology" for the Acadian Deportation against the British crown. A royal proclamation of December 9, 2003, established July 28 as the Commemoration of the Grand Dérangement. Perrin is the author of *Acadian Redemption*.

✦ Eddie Richard

Born in Lafayette Parish on September 14, 1923, Eddie
Richard was a founding member of the Confédération des
Familles Acadiennes, CAFA. He graduated from Southwestern
Louisiana Institute on the G.I. Bill following service in the
U.S. Air Force during WWII. He began his career with the
Boy Scouts of America. An activist and militant francophone,
Richard was district governor of the Rotary Club, member
of the Board of Directors of the Acadian Memorial, and one
of the principal organizers of the Congrés Mondial Acadien,
Louisiane 1999.

4.38 Eddie Richard

✦ William Arceneaux

4.39 William Arceneaux

William Arceneaux was born in Scott in 1941. He is
the founder of the Fondation Louisiane, devoted to the
development of French studies in Louisiana. Director of the
Foundation for Excellence in Louisiana Public Broadcasting,
Arceneaux has taught history at Tulane University and
Louisiana State University. He has been decorated as
Chevalier de l'Ordre de la Pléiade and Officier de l'Ordre
des Palmes Académiques of the French Republic. Arceneaux
was named president of CODOFIL in 2010.

Amanda Lafelur

4.40 Richard Guidry

Militant francophone Richard Guidry was the coordinator of bilingual education for the Louisiana Department of Education from 1980 to 2003. From Marais Michel near Gueydan, Guidry has worked unceasingly to integrate Louisiana French into the curriculum. He is the author of numerous short stories and plays that validate Cajun French and co-edited the *Dictionary of Louisiana French as Spoken in Cajun, Creole, and American Indian Communities.*

Cajun educators

At the beginning of the twentieth century, public education was a powerful force of the cultural and linguistic assimilation of the Cajun people. Following a compulsory education law of 1916, monolingual Cajun students were forced to attend schools where they were humiliated and punished for speaking French on the school grounds. Many teachers at the time were themselves Cajuns, part of an educated elite that had embraced Anglo-American culture. One hundred years later, however, Cajun educators are at the forefront of the efforts to preserve and promote the French language of Louisiana.

Amanda LaFleur : From Ville Platte in Evangeline Parish, Amanda Lafleur is an educator and author. She has designed French courses for secondary and university teaching that incorporate elements of the Cajun speech patterns. She is also co-editor of the *Dictionary of Louisiana French as Spoken in Cajun, Creole, and American Indian Communities.*

Nicole Boudreaux : Originally from France, Nicole Boudreaux arrived in Louisiana in 1970 as Foreign Associate Teacher in the CODOFIL program. Beginning in 1990, she worked for French immersion programs as a teacher and administrator. Boudreaux holds a Ph.D. in education from the University of Louisiana at Lafayette.

■ French immersion

Barry Ancelet

4.41   A French immersion class

In the 1960s, Cajun activists were responsible for the creation of CODOFIL, and the teaching of French was made obligatory at the elementary level throughout the state. "The schools destroyed the French language, the schools must revive it" was their motto. Since that time, many school districts have inaugurated French immersion programs.

The principle of French immersion is simple: Instead of teaching the secondary language as an independent subject, it is made the language of instruction, thereby creating an authentic need for the students to practice and to learn it.

The first French immersion class was founded in Lake Charles in Calcasieu Parish in 1986. Since that time, programs have been started in St. Martin, Assumption, Acadia, and Lafayette Parishes. The number of French immersion students has not stopped growing. During the 2010-2011 school year, there were thirty programs in twelve school districts with more than 3,600 students. The success of French immersion not only in teaching a second language but also as a means of improving education is incontestable.

CALL TO ACTION

Research and write a report on foreign language immersion in Louisiana. If possible interview students of foreign language immersion. Are there other foreign language immersion programs besides French being taught in Louisiana? How many foreign language students have been taught since the programs began? What do you think are the advantages of foreign language immersion? The disadvantages?

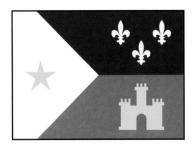

During the Acadian Bicentennial Celebration of 1955 com-
memorating the Deportation
of 1755, Allen Babineaux, an
activist from Lafayette, pro-
posed the creation of a Cajun
flag. His design was inspired
by the Acadian flag which he
had seen in Caraquet, New
Brunswick. Dr. Thomas Arceneaux, a dean at the University of Southwestern Louisiana
suggested an alternative. He
designed a flag with three sil-
ver fleur-de-lis on a blue field
to evoke the French heritage
of the Acadians, a gold cha-
teau to symbolize the Spanish
influence, and a gold star on
a white field to represent Our
Lady of the Assumption, the
patron of the Acadians.

Conclusion

Today's Cajuns are the result of a socio-cultural
evolution that began with their ancestral origins
in France. The colonial experience forged a new
identity among these peasant farmers and craftsmen
who settled in Acadie. The Acadians rather quickly
developed a sense of themselves that went beyond
their mother country. This identity was so strong
that it resisted the efforts of the English to shatter
the society by dispersing its citizens. Instead of
eliminating Acadia, the exile produced several
Acadias. The version that was established in Louisiana
continues to evolve and define itself, despite
systematic efforts for more than two centuries to

4.42 *Cajun World / Le monde cadien*, by Robert Dafford

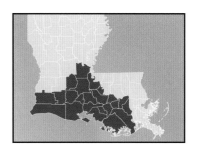

In 1963, a typographical error was made adding an "a" to the word "Acadian" by the Acadian Television Corporation in Lafayette. The station, KATC, immediately recognized that this would be a very attractive way to refer to the region. The name was used as a marketing strategy and resonated with the local population. The name appealed to ethnic Cajun pride and became very popular. In 1971, the Louisiana legislature created a twenty-two parish economic zone officially recognized as "Acadiana." Unified by their common Acadian heritage, the parishes of Acadiana stretch from Lafourche and St. Charles in the east to Calcasieu and Cameron in the west, and from the Gulf of Mexico to Avoyelles and Pointe Coupée in the north.

assimilate it, especially through attempts to eradicate its language. The Cajuns eventually found a place for themselves in the context of America's ethnic diversity. Many continue to sing and tell tales in French. With a strong Acadian base, they have also been formed by Louisiana's gumbo of influences. They have succeeded through it all in preserving their specificity in their cuisine, their music, their architecture, their sense of humor, their celebrations, and their industriousness, but most especially a survival strategy based on social cooperation, improvisation, and adaptation, all the while respecting a continuity between tradition and modernity.

– Barry Jean Ancelet

Glossary

aboiteau : The early Acadians developed a system of dikes that included a wooden box containing a trap door. At low tide, the trap would open, allowing fresh water to evacuate. The rising tide would close the trap, preventing salt water from reaching the drained marsh. The entire system, including the dike, the wooden trap, and the drained marsh are all referred to as "aboiteaux," although the term specifically refers to the wooden trap.

anse : literally "cove." A term used by the original Acadians to name settlements on the Attakapas prairie.

bal de maison : house dance

boucherie : Boucheries are family and communal events usually held in the fall. A hog is slaughtered. Meats and boudin sausage are prepared during a lively social gathering.

bousillage : a method of insulating early Acadian-style houses. A mixture of mud and Spanish moss was inserted in the spaces between the interior and exterior walls.

coulées : a small watercourse that feeds into a larger bayou

coups de main : literally "helping hand," the practice of mutual assistance by the family or community, usually for major projects such as barn rasing or house building.

coureurs : literally "runners." Participants in the traditional Courir du Mardi Gras (Mardi Gras run).

cuisine cadienne : Cajun cuisine

filé : ground up sassafras used to thicken gumbo

Flottille de Nantes : The flotilla of Nantes, comprising seven ships, sailed from France to Louisiana transporting nearly the entire exiled Acadian community. The ships sailed from May to October of 1785.

garçonnière : bedroom for unmarried boys in the traditional Acadian-style house. The garçonnière is an attic space reached by a flight of small stairs on the front porch.

gateaux de sirop : syrup cake

Grand Dérangement : literally the "Great Annoyance." Normally, the term "dérangement" refers to something incommodious, but certainly not tragic. It is not without irony that the Acadians referred to their forced exile as the "Great Annoyance." The term has been translated in official documents as the "Great Upheaval," which does not do justice to the sardonic quality of the original expression. By referring to their Deportation as an "annoyance," the Acadians made light of the terribly devastating nature of the Deportation and years of exile.

gratons : fried bits of pork skin. During the traditional Cadien boucherie, the rinds of pork skin are cut into dice-sized pieces and deep fried.

guérisseurs : folk healers

la chasse et la pêche : hunting and fishing

La chanson des Mardis gras :

The Mardi Gras song

The Mardi Gras come from England,
All around, all around the hub.
They come once a year to ask for charity
Even if it is just a skinny chicken
And three or four ears of corn.

The Mardi Gras are not brigands
They are just beggars,
Captain Sosthene asks
Yes, of each master and each mistress
Permission to enter and beg.

The Mardi Gras are on a long voyage
All around, all around the hub.
They come once a year to ask for charity
Even if it is just a potato,
A potato and some gratons.

les courses de chevaux : horse racing

marais : literally "swamp." On the Cajun prairie, the marais held water permanently and their names were used as place names, such as Marais Michel or Marais Bouleur.

planche debout : literally "upright plank," a form of siding using cypress planks found on the early Acadian-style house.

platins : low lying cavities on the Cajun prairie that frequently held water

poteaux en terre : literally "post in ground," a method of construction for the early Acadian-style house

ramasseries : harvesting practiced by the family or community group

Religion Catholique : Catholic religion

traiteurs : faith healers

veillées : social evenings including conversation, storytelling, singing, and dancing

Bibliography

ANCELET, Barry Jean, Jay EDWARDS, and Glen PITRE. *Cajun Country*, Jackson: University Press of Mississippi, 1991.

ARSENAULT, Bona. *Histoire des Acadiens*. Québec: Conseil de la vie française en Amérique, 1966.

BASQUE, Maurice. *Des hommes de pouvoir: histoire d'Otho Robichaud et de sa famille, notables acadiens de Port-Royal et de Néguac*. Néguac: Société historique de Néguac, 1996.

BASQUE, Maurice, Nicole BARRIEAU and Stéphanie CÔTÉ. *L'Acadie de l'Atlantique*. Moncton: Société nationale de l'Acadie et Centre d'études acadiennes, Centre international de recherche et de documentation de la francophonie, Année francophone internationale, 1999.

BASQUE, Maurice, and Jacques Paul COUTURIER (dir.). *Les territoires de l'identité: perspectives acadiennes et françaises, XVIIᵉ-XXᵉ siècles*. Moncton: Chaire d'études acadiennes, 2005.

BELLIVEAU, Pierre. *French Neutrals in Massachusetts, The Story of Acadians Rounded up by Soldiers from Massachusetts and Their Captivity in the Bay Province, 1755-1766*. Boston: Kirk S. Giffen, 1972.

BERNARD, Shane K. *The Cajuns, Americanization of a People*. Jackson: University Press of Mississippi, 2003.

——.*Cajuns and Their Acadian Ancestors, A Young Reader's History*. Jackson: University Press of Mississippi, 2008.

BRASSEAUX, Carl A. *The Founding of New Acadia*. Baton Rouge: Louisiana State University Press, 1987.

——. *Acadian to Cajun, Transformation of a People, 1803-1877*. Jackson: University Press of Mississippi, 1992.

BUTLER, Gary R. *Histoire et traditions orales des Franco-Acadiens de Terre-Neuve*. Sillery: Septentrion, 1995.

CAZAUX, Yves. *L'Acadie, Histoire des Acadiens, du XVIIᵉ siècle à nos jours*. Paris: Albin Michel, 1992.

COLLECTIF. *Les défricheurs d'eau: le village*

historique acadien, aperçu de l'histoire matérielle de l'Acadie du Nouveau-Brunswick. Moncton: Éditions de la Francophonie, 2003.

CORMIER, Yves. Les aboiteaux en Acadie: hier et aujourd'hui. Moncton: Chaire d'études acadiennes, 1990.

——. Dictionnaire du français acadien. Saint-Lauren: Fides, 1999.

DAIGLE, Jean (dir.). L'Acadie des Maritimes: études thématiques des débuts à nos jours, Moncton: Chaire d'études acadiennes, 1993.

DEVEAU, Alphonse J. Valentin Landry (1844-1919): à la barre de L'Évangéline – At the Helm of L'Évangéline. Moncton: Éditions d'Acadie; Memramcook: Société du Monument Lefebvre, 1992.

DEVEAU, Alphonse J., and Sally ROSS. Les Acadiens de la Nouvelle-Écosse, hier et aujourd'hui. Moncton: Éditions d'Acadie, 1995.

DIONNE, Raoul. La colonisation acadienne au Nouveau-Brunswick, 1760-1860 : données sur les concessions de terres. Moncton: Chaire d'études acadiennes, 1989.

EDMONDS, David C. Yankee Autumn in Acadiana. Lafayette: Acadiana Press, 1979.

FONTENEAU, Jean-Marie. Les Acadiens, citoyens de l'Atlantique. Rennes: Ouest-France, 1996.

GIRAUD, Marcel. L'histoire de la Louisiane française, 4 Volumes. Paris: Presses Universitaires de France, 1953.

GRIFFITHS, Naomi E. S. The Contexts of Acadian History, 1686-1784. Montréal: McGill-Queen's University Press, 1992.

——. From Migrant to Acadian: A North American Border People, 1604-1755. Moncton: Institut canadien de recherche en politiques et administration publiques; Montréal: McGill-Queen's University Press, 2005.

LANDRY, Nicolas, and Nicole LANG. Histoire de l'Acadie. Sillery: Septentrion, 2001.

LEBLANC, Dudley. The Acadian Miracle. Lafayette: Evangeline Publishing Company, 1966 (revised and expanded edition of The True Story of the Acadians, published in 1927).

LEBLANC, F. S. Cajun-Bred Running Horses.

Lafayette: Acadian Press, 1978.

LEBLANC, Ronnie-Gilles (dir.). *Du Grand Dérangement à la Déportation: nouvelles perspectives historiques*. Moncton: Chaire d'études acadiennes, 2005.

LÉGER, Lauraine. Critical edition of *Chez les anciens Acadiens: causeries du grand-père Antoine* d'André -T. Bourque. Moncton: Chaire d'études acadiennes, 1994.

LOWRIE, Walter. *Early Settlers of Louisiana as Taken from Land Claims in the Eastern District of the Orleans Territory*. Washington: Duff Green, 1834; Southern Historical Press, 1986.

MAILLET, Antonine. *Pélagie-la-Charrette*. Montréal: Leméac, 1979.

PICHETTE, Robert. *Napoléon III, l'Acadie et le Canada Français*. Moncton: Éditions d'Acadie, 1998.

RUMILLY, Robert. *L'Acadie anglaise (1713-1755)*. Montréal: Fides, 1983.

SURETTE, Paul. *Atlas de l'établissement des Acadiens aux Trois-Rivières du Chignectou 1660-1755*. Moncton: Éditions d'Acadie, 1996.

VANDERLINDEN, Jacques. *Se marier en Acadie française, XVIIe et XVIIIe siècles*. Moncton: Éditions d'Acadie, 1998; Chaire d'études acadiennes, Université de Moncton, coll. Mouvange.

List of Illustrations

List of Maps